ONE PERSON,
NO ★ VOTE

Also by Carol Anderson with Tonya Bolden

We Are Not Yet Equal: Understanding Our Racial Divide

A YOUNG ADULT ADAPTATION

ONE PERSON, NO ★ VOTE

HOW NOT ALL VOTERS ARE TREATED EQUALLY

CAROL ANDERSON

WITH TONYA BOLDEN

BLOOMSBURY

NEW YORK   LONDON   OXFORD   NEW DELHI   SYDNEY

BLOOMSBURY YA
Bloomsbury Publishing Inc., part of Bloomsbury Publishing Plc
1385 Broadway, New York, NY 10018

BLOOMSBURY and the Diana logo are trademarks of
Bloomsbury Publishing Plc

First published in the United States of America in September 2019
by Bloomsbury YA

One Person, No Vote: How Not All Voters Are Treated Equally is a young adult adaptation of
One Person, No Vote: How Voter Suppression Is Destroying Our Democracy by Carol Anderson,
first published in 2018 by Bloomsbury USA

Bloomsbury books may be purchased for business or promotional use.
For information on bulk purchases please contact Macmillan Corporate and
Premium Sales Department at specialmarkets@macmillan.com

Library of Congress Cataloging-in-Publication Data
available upon request
ISBN 978-1-5476-0107-3 (hardcover) • ISBN 978-1-5476-0153-0 (e-book)

Book design by Kate Gartner
Typeset by Westchester Publishing Services
Printed and bound in the U.S.A. by Berryville Graphics Inc., Berryville, Virginia
2 4 6 8 10 9 7 5 3 1

All papers used by Bloomsbury Publishing Plc are natural, recyclable products
made from wood grown in well-managed forests. The manufacturing processes
conform to the environmental regulations of the country of origin.

To find out more about our authors and books visit www.bloomsbury.com
and sign up for our newsletters.

To all of the voting rights warriors and activists who have fought and continue to fight to protect Democracy

CONTENTS

ONE PERSON,
NO ★ VOTE

PROLOGUE

HMM . . .

It was a mystery worthy of master crime writer Raymond Chandler.

And the mystery was this: On November 8, 2016, black Americans did not show up at the polls.

It was like a day of absence.

Of a mostly black district in Milwaukee, Wisconsin, one reporter was told that folks there had virtually boycotted the election because they "simply saw no affirmative reason to vote for Hillary. Some saw her as corrupt; others noted that they had not seen their economic situation improved during the Obama years."

Another journalist concluded that because Hillary Clinton lacked the ability, charisma, or magic to keep Barack Obama's coalition together, "African-American, Latino and younger voters failed to show up at the polls in sufficient numbers." As proof of black people's coolness toward Hillary Clinton, journalists pointed to the much greater turnout for Barack Obama in 2008 and 2012.

Yes, nationwide black voter turnout had dropped by nearly 17 percent. What's more, less than half of Latino and Asian American voters went to the polls. The tide of black, Latino, and Asian American voters that had carried Obama into the White House in 2008 and kept him there for a second term had visibly ebbed.

But, you see, blacks, Latinos, and Asian Americans did not simply refuse to vote. Republican legislatures and governors had systematically blocked millions from the polls.

Why?

To survive.

The GOP's overwhelmingly white constituency was becoming an ever smaller share of the voting public and the party wasn't attracting legions of people of color because of its inability to craft policies that speak to an increasingly diverse nation.

Rather than reform—change its ways, its outlook—the GOP decided to disenfranchise—to deprive Democrat-leaning people of their right to vote.

One Person, No Vote is the story of these desperate, dastardly, and most undemocratic measures—and the history behind them.

★ PART ONE ★

A HISTORY OF DISENFRANCHISEMENT

After Reconstruction, some black Americans obtained positions in the government. But their power soon dwindled as white Americans worked against them.

1

BUBBLES IN A BAR OF SOAP

THE MILLIONS OF VOTES *AND* VOTERS THAT DISAP-
peared in 2016 were a long time in the making.

The drive to disenfranchise black people, in particular, is
best understood by going back to strides toward a real democracy. A government, as Abraham Lincoln said in his Gettysburg
Address, "of the people, by the people, for the people."

This moment came after the Civil War, during Reconstruction. It brought, among other things, the 1865 Thirteenth
Amendment to the US Constitution (slavery abolished), the 1868
Fourteenth Amendment (black citizenship cemented), and the
1870 Fifteenth Amendment (black men gained the national vote).

But a more democratic America was anathema to a multi-
tude of white people.

Reconstruction, which ended in 1877, saw scores of black
men in the political arena and in government. Black artisans and
entrepreneurs, laborers and lawyers, mechanics and ministers

became postmasters, sheriffs, marshals, councilmen, commissioners, state legislators, secretaries of state. A handful were lieutenant governors. More than a dozen served in the US Congress.

And so many did so much good. For example, one black South Carolina legislator remarked, black men helped to craft "the laws relative to finance, the building of penal and charitable institutions, and, greatest of all, the establishment of the public school system." Yet the myth of incompetent, disastrous so-called black rule dominated. Said one newspaper editor in the early 1870s: "No negro is fit to make laws for white people."

> "Many Texans refused to accept the fact that the Negro was 'free and equal,' and stopped at nothing to prevent him from enjoying civic and political rights."
>
> —Maud Cuney Hare in her biography of her father, Norris Wright Cuney, a leading black Lone Star State activist, entrepreneur, and politician during Reconstruction

After Reconstruction, legions of white people did their utmost to ensure white rule—to keep black men from voting, to prevent black America from having any real political power. (While some black men did hold political office after Reconstruction, the numbers dwindled and dwindled.)

Black voter suppression really ramped up in 1890 when the Magnolia State passed what became known as the Mississippi Plan: a dizzying array of poll taxes; literacy tests; understanding clauses (which officials used to justify registering some white illiterate people who they claimed understood the information read to them); newfangled voter registration rules; and "good character" clauses. All were racially discriminatory, but they were pitched as simply a way to bring "integrity" to the polls.

Virginia state senator Carter Glass, like many other white politicians, swooned at the thought of bringing the Mississippi Plan to his state. During Virginia's 1901–2 state constitutional convention, Glass championed a plan that would "eliminate the darkey as a political factor in this state in less than five years."

"Will it not be done by fraud and discrimination?" asked a fellow delegate.

"By fraud, no. By discrimination, yes," replied Glass. "Discrimination! Why, that is precisely what we propose. That, exactly, is what this Convention was elected for—to discriminate to the very extremity of permissible action under the limitations of the Federal Constitution, with a view to the elimination of every negro voter who can be gotten rid of, legally, without materially impairing the numerical strength of the white electorate."

But the drive to wipe out the black vote would hurt poor and illiterate white people. And for many of those in power, that was just fine.

For some it was the point.

Mississippi's Eaton Bowers, who served in Congress in the early 1900s, later said that his state's new constitution had disenfranchised "the ignorant and vicious white" voter along with black voters. He stated that Mississippi's eligible voters were "now confined to those, and to those alone, who are qualified by intelligence and character for the proper and patriotic exercise of this great franchise." While there was a steady erosion of white voters, the collapse of black voter turnout was precipitous.

In 1946—fifty-six years after the Mississippi Plan was unveiled—Mississippi Senator Theodore Bilbo, one of the most virulent racists to walk the halls of Congress, boasted of the chicanery. "What keeps 'em [blacks] from voting is section 244 of the [Mississippi] Constitution of 1890. . . . It says that a man to register must be able to read and explain the Constitution or explain the Constitution when read to him." Senator James Zachariah George, the "father" of that 1890 state constitution, bragged Bilbo, crafted a document few white men and no black people could explain.

The literacy test and understanding clause were tailor-made for societies that systematically refused to educate millions of their citizens and ensured that the bulk of the population remained functionally illiterate. By 1940, more than half of all black adults in Mississippi had fewer than five years of formal education. Almost 12 percent had no schooling whatsoever. The figures were worse in South Carolina, Louisiana, Georgia, and Alabama. During World War II, for example, Louisiana spent almost four times as much per capita on white elementary schoolchildren as on black ones. What's more, for most of the twentieth century, many Jim Crow school systems did not have high schools for black teens.

Deliberate underfunding of black schools was critical to the disenfranchising success of literacy tests.

Along with giving would-be black voters complicated passages of constitutions to explain, registrars concocted other ways

ANALYZE THIS!

A sample passage from Alabama's constitution, which could be part of a literacy test that a would-be black voter might have to read and explain circa 1965:

SECTION 260

The income arising from the sixteenth section trust fund, the surplus revenue fund, until it is called for by the United States government, and the funds enumerated in sections 257 and 258 of this Constitution, together with a special annual tax of thirty cents on each one hundred dollars of taxable property in this state, which the legislature shall levy, shall be applied to the support and maintenance of the public schools, and it shall be the duty of the legislature to increase the public school fund from time to time as the necessity therefor and the condition of the treasury and the resources of the state may justify; provided, that nothing herein contained shall be so construed as to authorize the legislature to levy in any one year a greater rate of state taxation for all purposes, including schools, than sixty-five cents on each one hundred dollars' worth of taxable property; and provided further, that nothing herein contained shall prevent the legislature from first providing for the payment of the bonded indebtedness of the state and interest thereon out of all the revenue of the state.

to stymie black voting. Black coal miner Leon Alexander learned this firsthand in the late 1940s when he went to the courthouse in Jefferson County, Alabama, to register to vote. Once in the registrar's office, Alexander stood at the counter waiting and waiting while the registrar made a big show of deliberately ignoring him. In contrast, when white folks showed up, the man promptly assisted them.

Leon Alexander stood his ground, refused to leave.

"What you want boy?" the registrar finally asked.

"I wants to register to vote," replied Alexander.

The registrar gave him the paperwork, then, after Alexander completed it, the man balled it up and tossed it into the trash can. "You disqualified," he said. "You didn't answer the question."

It took the intervention of three white officials in the local United Mine Workers union, who got Governor Jim Folsom involved, before Leon Alexander was finally registered to vote. And even then the registrar tried to have the last laugh. He didn't add Alexander's name to the official list of eligible voters, so that although he was registered, he couldn't cast a ballot. That required another intervention: one of those white allies telephoned and demanded that the registrar include Leon Alexander's name on the list.

What happened to Leon Alexander occurred over and over in registrars' offices across the South. What's more, as historian David C. Colby pointed out, "registrars asked blacks irrelevant questions."

Questions like this: "How many bubbles are in a bar of soap?"

And then there was the poll tax.

The separate entrances to a café are indicative of Jim Crow–era segregation in the South.

2

POLL TAX BLUES

IN THEIR 1940 ARTICLE "DISENFRANCHISEMENT BY Means of the Poll Tax," scholars Dan Nimmo and Clifton McCleskey explained that "the revival of the poll tax after the Civil War was intended not so much to disenfranchise the Negro as to place him again under the white man's domination, since failure to pay the tax was made prima facie [proof positive] evidence of vagrancy."

Black people charged with vagrancy (often falsely) could be jailed and even auctioned off to slave away on some white person's plantation or other enterprise. As Nimmo and McCleskey further explained, a poor black person "who desired to stay off the chain gang was . . . forced to place himself under the protection of a white man who would pay the tax for him."

It was only years later, during the rise of Jim Crow, that the poll tax was deliberately used to choke off the black vote when many states required all age-eligible males to pay an annual fee in order to vote. (This would also apply to women after they gained the national vote in 1920 through the Nineteenth Amendment.)

Poll tax proponents claimed that it sprang from noble intent: holding elections cost money and extra funds were necessary to meet the needs of democracy. Some also said the poll tax provided additional revenue for public schools. Still others draped themselves in the flag and maintained that a person who groused about the poll tax didn't deserve the vote.

But for many people the poll tax, ranging from $1 to $2, was no trifling thing. Not if you were poor, as many Southerners were. Many of them were sharecroppers. In his 1940 article "Suffrage in the South: The Poll Tax," George C. Stoney noted that in Mississippi, the average farm family's income was "less than $100 a year." The poll tax would eat up almost 2 percent of the family's income. If there were two would-be voters in that household, the poll tax would eat up nearly 4 percent. If three or four would-be voters . . .

What's more, for many states, the poll tax was cumulative. For every year a person was eligible to vote, a payment was due. So if, after twenty years of not voting or having been unable to vote, a person, say, in Alabama in 1944 was finally able to pay, he or she would need to cough up not $1.50 to do so but rather $30. In 1944 a person could buy several pairs of shoes for family members with those thirty dollars.

The poll tax came with yet another turnoff. In most states, it was due *months* before the election. Said white liberal politician Maury Maverick to George C. Stoney: "paying a poll tax in February to vote in November is to most folks in Texas like buying a ticket to a show nine months ahead of time, and before you know who's playing or really what the thing is all about. It is easy to forget to do, too."

And say a black person could afford to pay the poll tax, there was the intimidation factor. You see, it was members of law enforcement who collected the poll tax. White sheriffs and sheriffs' deputies were notorious in the black community for their brutality. A 1965 Commission on Civil Rights report told of a sheriff who "instructed his deputies to require all persons paying poll taxes for the first time to apply to him personally." This was in Tallahatchie County, Mississippi, where "most whites but few Negroes had registered to vote."

There were other devious moves in poll tax systems. Mississippi, for instance, required people to produce receipts for two years of poll taxes in order to vote. The tilt in the playing field was apparent when arch-segregationist Theodore Bilbo's political operatives worked with election officials to handle the difficulty of keeping track of multiyear receipts. His all-white constituency's "receipts are not only bought for them but are kept on file, issued on election day, re-collected and saved for the next year," wrote George C. Stoney.

The political machines in Texas did something similar. They would "buy up as many poll tax receipts as they [could], . . . keep them on file and pass them out . . . on election day—with instructions, of course, and an extra dollar or so for sweetenin'," a man told George Stoney.

It was a total debasement and corruption of democracy, and it worked. During World War II, the overall voter turnout in seven poll tax states was an estimated 3 percent for the midterm election. The 1944 presidential election was only marginally better. The poll tax states had about an 18 percent turnout rate, as compared with the nearly 69 percent national average.

The poll tax died a slow death: abolished in North Carolina in 1920, in Louisiana in 1934, in Florida in 1937, in Georgia in 1945, in Tennessee in 1951, and in South Carolina in 1952. Then, finally in 1964, through the Twenty-fourth Amendment, the poll tax was outlawed in federal elections from sea to shining sea. Meanwhile . . .

Added to literacy tests, understanding clauses, and the poll taxes was the skullduggery of the white primary.

Dr. Lawrence A. Nixon was the plaintiff in *Nixon v. Herndon*, a case that inaugurated a decades-long struggle through the US Supreme Court to gain voter equality prior to the Voting Rights Act.

3

ONLY DEMOCRATS NEED APPLY

SO DESPISED WAS THE PARTY OF ABRAHAM LINCOLN, as the Republican Party was known—the party responsible for the Thirteenth, Fourteenth, and Fifteenth Amendments—that from Reconstruction until 1968 the South was a one-party system.

Only Democrats need apply.

Several of the states, therefore, began to discern that one way to skirt the Fifteenth Amendment was to tinker with the primary election, during which the Democratic candidate was chosen. Because the South was a one-party region, whoever won in the spring would certainly be the victor in November. And just so long as the all-important and decisive primary was a whites-only affair, the results would be foreordained.

People thought that they could get away with this because in 1921 the US Supreme Court had ruled in *Newberry v. United States* that the federal government, and, thus, the US Constitution itself, had no authority over the conduct of primary elections in the states.

With no federal interference and a one-party system, the white primary became a masterful way to "emasculate politically the entire body of Negro voters," wrote Leo Alilunas in his 1940s article "The Rise of the 'White Primary' Movement as a Means of Barring the Negro from the Polls." Come the general election, blacks who defied other methods of disenfranchisement, such as poll taxes and literacy tests, could vote if they wished—in what was by then an irrelevant and perfunctory election.

Except black people fought back. Over the span of twenty years, they launched four separate lawsuits that went all the way to the US Supreme Court. Texas was the main site of this battle, because while all eleven states of the old Confederacy had the white primary, the Lone Star State did it in "a more brutally direct fashion." Its 1923 statute expressly forbid anyone but whites from voting in the Democratic primary.

That was too explicit even for a US Supreme Court that had previously decided that the poll tax and the literacy test were constitutional in an 1898 decision in the case *Williams v. Mississippi*. After reviewing Texas's white primary law, and seeing such an explicit violation of the Fourteenth Amendment's equal protection clause, the court was unanimous and unequivocal: "It seems to us hard to imagine a more direct and obvious infringement of the Fourteenth Amendment," said Justice Oliver W. Holmes Jr., delivering the High Court's decision in the case *Nixon v. Herndon*, a case decided in March 1927.

Texas was, however, undaunted. Satisfied that the court

hadn't questioned whether the white primary actually violated the Fifteenth Amendment right to vote, the legislature simply redrafted the statute to turn the Democratic Party into a private organization—one to which the state just happened to delegate the authority to hold a primary. The point of this ruse was perfectly clear. In the *United States v. Cruikshank* decision, almost fifty years earlier in 1876, the US Supreme Court had established that private actors were "immune from the strictures of the Fourteenth and Fifteenth Amendments."

Again, blacks challenged Texas's law, and again they prevailed—though this time by only a 5–4 decision in *Nixon v. Condon*, decided in May 1932. The statute, justices ruled, was unconstitutional because the so-called private Democratic Party received its authority directly from the state. Therefore, it was not a "private" actor at all but an agent of the State of Texas.

Lawmakers in Austin soldiered on, unfazed, cleverly picking up on the part of the court's ruling that laid out that African Americans "could be excluded from primaries" by putting the authority for that exclusion in the state Democratic convention. Less than a month after the *Nixon v. Condon* decision, the Democratic Party called a statewide convention and passed a resolution "restricting membership in the Party plus participation in party primaries to white citizens of Texas."

Once again, the state had effectively eliminated black Americans and Mexican Americans (this was, after all, Texas) from having any real voice in determining their representatives in government or the policies that would affect their lives. And so in 1935, blacks sued Texas for a third time. Only this time, the Supreme Court held that the Democratic primary was now a private matter. An organization had the right to choose the qualifications for membership, and that, according to the Supreme Court, is exactly what the Democratic Party did. Therefore, the State of Texas had not violated black people's rights.

Ridding this nation of the white primary now looked impossible, but a subsequent US Supreme Court decision in 1940 finally "pierced the façade of legality which had shielded primaries from the reach of Federal laws regulating the conduct of elections," wrote Thurgood Marshall in his penetrating 1957 essay "The Rise and Collapse of the 'White Democratic Primary.'"

This landmark case from Louisiana, *United States v. Classic* (1941), erased much of the ambiguity about how far the Fourteenth and Fifteenth Amendments could reach into the election process. "If a state law made the primary an integral part of the election machinery and if the primary did effectively control the choice of the elected official then Congress had the right and the duty to regulate and control such primaries," explained historian Darlene Clark Hine of the High Court's thinking.

That clarity created a legal basis for the fourth white primary case, *Smith v. Allwright* (1944). A black Texan wrote, "One thing is certain, as a result of the Classic case . . . the tables are turned . . . now the Negroes are on top." In an 8–1 decision, the Supreme Court affirmed that sentiment when it ruled that the white primary, although supposedly a private affair, was central to the election process and, therefore, fell under the domain of federal law and the US Constitution. Marshall was overjoyed that the High Court had finally "looked behind the law and ferreted out the trickery."

But the shenanigans continued.

South Carolina decided to maintain the white primary while at the same time purging its books of all election laws. The rationale was this: with nothing written down, there was nothing that the courts could find in violation of the Fourteenth or Fifteenth Amendments.

Not to be outdone, Texas offered up yet another scheme, this one with a pre-primary in the guise of the all-white, private Jaybird Democratic Association, that would then feed into the Democratic primary without any official machinery involved—no election laws, public funding, or certification by the party. The state reasoned that because this was supposedly before any real election activities took place and there appeared to be a firewall between this private club and government officialdom, Texas could avoid running afoul of the US Constitution. In 1953, in *Terry v. Adams*, the Supreme Court disagreed, saying that the scheme in whatever guise was unconstitutional. With that, it finally and completely drove a stake through the heart of the white primary.

But Southern racists had yet another arrow in their quiver.

A black citizen near a sign associated with a Eugene Talmadge rally. Talmadge's aim was to ensure that blacks were not considered qualified to vote.

4

AND DON'T FORGET
THE MATCHES

WHAT STATES COULD NOT ACCOMPLISH BY LAW, they were more than willing to achieve by violence. Attacks on black Americans in Colfax, Louisiana (1873), Wilmington, North Carolina (1898), and Ocoee, Florida (1920)—just to name a few—resulted in the loss of hundreds of lives simply because whites were enraged that black people had voted. As states encouraged or winked at the murders, as killers stepped over the bodies and gobbled up victims' land and other property, black political power evaporated in a hail of gunfire and flames. This violence continued well into the twentieth century.

In 1946, former Georgia governor Eugene Talmadge knew that World War II had lit a political fire in black America with its Double V Campaign—Victory for Democracy abroad *and* at home: the number of black Georgians registered to vote had skyrocketed from 20,000 in 1944 to 135,000 just two years later—a year after Georgia got rid of the poll tax. During his run to regain the governor's office, Talmadge vowed to reinstate the white primary, welcomed the endorsement of the Ku Klux Klan, and pledged to keep black people in their place.

Talmadge's followers carried out a major purge of the voting rolls, especially in the rural counties. They also engaged in acts of intimidation such as cross burnings. And Talmadge gave his blessing to waves of anti-black violence. A World War II veteran, Maceo Snipes, was one of the first to get caught in the tide of state-sponsored lynching.

Black veterans were particular targets throughout the country because their sense of rights and racial justice had grown especially acute during the battles of World War II. Snipes had already put his life on the line for democracy. In 1946, he was willing to do it again.

When the 1946 primary rolled around—the first since the US Supreme Court's *Smith v. Allwright* decision—Maceo Snipes was not about to sit out the election in Taylor County, Georgia, where whites had already posted a sign on black churches that read: "The first Negro to vote will never vote again."

Undeterred, in July 1946, Maceo Snipes cast his ballot, the only black person in the county to do so. A few days later, white men showed up at Snipes's house and demanded that he step outside.

He did and was shot.

Maceo's mother ran out of the house and got him to the hospital, where he lay in a room the size of a closet unattended for six hours bleeding, just bleeding. This strong man, this veteran, lingered for two more days, but the damage was too extensive, the medical treatment too slow, and Georgia's hate too deep.

So was Mississippi's.

During the 1946 primary in Mississippi, Senator Theodore Bilbo riled up his "red-blooded Anglo-Saxon" followers with orders that "the best way to keep [black people] from voting . . . [was to] do it the night before the election." In the run-up to the election, if any black person sought to organize to vote, "use the tar and feathers," he advised, "and don't forget the matches."

In some cases, when would-be black voters tried to register to vote they were simply turned away. In others, officials taunted them, demanding that they "paint . . . their faces white" if they wanted to vote in the white primary. In still other cases, people were just beaten.

After he was physically assaulted, V. R. Collier, president of the National Association for the Advancement of Colored People (NAACP) branch in Gulfport, Mississippi, turned to the FBI for help, only to be told that the bureau didn't protect; it investigated. When Collier called the US attorney in Jackson, he was told to contact the FBI.

Intimidation and violence did a heck of a job keeping black Americans from the polls. Over and over those who tried to register to vote were photographed by the police, were harassed and threatened by gun-toting, pickup-driving toughs. They received visits from sheriffs and endured arrests on trumped-up charges that led to jail time or exorbitant fines.

Some Startling Stats

• By 1940 a mere 3 percent of black people eligible to vote in the South were registered to do so.

• In 1867, the percentage of black people registered to vote in Mississippi was 66.9 percent. By 1955, it was 4.3 percent.

• In 1896 Louisiana had more than 130,000 black people registered to vote. By 1904 that number was down to 1,342.

• The number of black people registered to vote in Alabama plunged from 180,000 in 1900 to less than 3,000 in 1903.

Denying the vote to millions of American citizens was so deeply rooted in the fabric of the nation, twisted into the mechanics of government, and embedded in the political strategy and thinking of powerful government officials that this clear affront to democracy was not going to change on its own. Fortunately, local resistance and global condemnation combined to take America to the brink of democracy.

Soviet media played on American racism and developed propaganda demonstrating its evils.

5

HERE COMES THE VRA

STARTING IN 1947, THE UNITED STATES FOUND itself in a pitched battle for global leadership against the Soviet Union, aka the USSR (Union of Soviet Socialist Republics), a federation of fifteen republics, with Moscow, the capital of the Russian republic, the center of power.

Two superpowers.

Two warring ideologies (state control of everything versus capitalism).

Two economies ("command" or government controlled versus free market).

Two nations with enough nuclear weapons to destroy the planet several times over. A head-on confrontation would result in Mutually Assured Destruction (MAD). Instead, the USA and the USSR fought a series of proxy wars in Asia, Africa, and Latin America. This means they chose sides in civil wars—including

Korea (1950–1953) and Vietnam (1955–1975)—arming and financing combatants aligned with their ideologies.

There was also the propaganda war. The Soviet Union prided itself on meeting the material needs—housing, employment, health care—of its people. The people paid a steep price for those basics, including the loss of both freedom of speech and freedom of the press. The Soviet weakness played directly into the Americans' strength: democracy.

But wait a minute.

With Jim Crow on the throne, America's vaunted democratic ideals became an Achilles' heel. The Soviets broadcast this hypocrisy at every turn.

Each lynching, each bombing of a black home or business, each miscarriage of justice became grist for the Soviet Union's propaganda mill. One article in the Communist party–controlled Soviet press laid out the "numerous examples of racial terrorism," in the USA, from the lynching of Emmett Till (1955) to "the brutal persecution" of Autherine Lucy, the first black student at the University of Alabama (1956). While such stories poked holes in the American narrative of democracy, what happened in Little Rock blew a hole through it.

White resistance to the *Brown v. Board of Education of Topeka, Kansas* decision (1954), in which the US Supreme Court ruled segregated public schooling unconstitutional, was fiery, furious, fevered. It erupted most visibly in Little Rock, Arkansas, in 1957, when nine black honor students sought to desegregate Central High School. The venom and violence these teenagers faced was seen around the world.

It was horrible publicity.

And the Soviet Union did not miss a beat. "National guard soldiers and policemen armed to the teeth bar Negro children from entering the schools, threaten them with bayonets and tear-gas bombs and encourage hooligans to engage in violence with impunity," declared one newspaper.

Little Rock also caught the attention of nations the United States wanted firmly allied with the West. Henry Cabot Lodge, US ambassador to the United Nations, wrote President Dwight Eisenhower that at the UN he could "see clearly the harm that [Little Rock is] doing. . . . More than two-thirds of the world is non-white and the reactions of [their] representatives is easy to see."

The *Times of India* ran a front-page story titled, "Armed Men Cordon Off White School: Racial Desegregation in Arkansas Prevented." Similar articles dominated the news in Egypt, Tanganyika, and elsewhere.

The United States had zero credibility in the eyes of many around the world. Don't be fooled, the Soviet Union warned: the US goal was to export Jim Crow, not democracy. "American racism and its savage practice of cruel persecution and abuse of minorities is . . . the true nature of the American 'democracy' which the United States is trying to foist on other countries and peoples."

Black Americans were well aware of the global Cold War context of their struggle for true freedom. But it was a series of local insurgencies in the black community erupting across the South that gave that uprising the aura of a "movement." Recognizing the importance of the media in documenting and broadcasting confrontations, black leaders in Montgomery, Atlanta,

Birmingham, and other cities doubled down on a nonviolent strategy to call out the evil that black Americans faced when trying to vote, go to good schools, shop, dine, and just live.

Although it came to the realization slowly, the US government now faced a nation-defining decision. America was caught between, on one hand, the power of the Southern Democrats in Congress, whose inordinate political strength and control of key committees was based on their ability to win reelection after reelection because of massive disenfranchisement; and on the other, the missionary-like belief that the USA was the champion of democracy and freedom.

President Eisenhower's solution was the 1957 Civil Rights Act, the first civil rights bill in eighty-odd years. This bill created the Commission on Civil Rights, upgraded the Department of Justice's section on civil rights to a division, and authorized the US attorney general to sue those violating the voting rights of American citizens.

The core of the 1957 Civil Rights Act gave the US Department of Justice (DOJ) the authority to sue jurisdictions (cities or towns) that blocked citizens from voting based on the color of their skin. Sounds good—but the lawsuit mechanism had a number of problems.

First, DOJ lawsuits would be a reaction to voting rights violations, not a preventative. In other words, the "crime" had to occur before the DOJ stepped in. This meant that skewed election results, where a racist candidate assumed office because black citizens had been systematically disenfranchised, could affect years of policy and lawmaking while the long, drawn-out court process slowly unfolded.

After investigation, these DOJ lawsuits would take, on average, an additional 17.8 months between the trial and ruling, and then another year for the appeal if the ruling went against the plaintiff.

And there was another "if."

If the registrar who was the named defendant in the lawsuit left office at any point during this process (a common ploy), then the case was thrown out.

Added to all this: DOJ attorneys often faced white judges and all-white juries hostile to black people. The kicker—the DOJ was reluctant to pursue these cases with any true vigor in the first place.

On May 6, 1960, President Eisenhower signed another civil rights act designed to strengthen the 1957 one. Among other things, it removed the two-year limit of the Commission on Civil Rights and established penalties for people interfering with someone's attempt to register to vote. But this was still not enough. The unrelenting pressure of the Civil Rights Movement, however, meant that America's weak response to disenfranchisement would not go unchallenged. In Alabama's Marion, Lowndes, and Dallas Counties, years of nonviolent protest led to a cinematic explosion on Sunday, March 7, 1965, on the Edmund Pettus Bridge in Selma.

As peaceful marchers ran into the hailstorm of Alabama state troopers and sheriff Jim Clark's deputies, news cameras captured the horror of tear gas, barbed-wire bullwhips, and police on horseback trampling people. Millions around the nation and the world sat in stunned silence, almost traumatized by the spectacle, a sickening scene that would become known as Bloody Sunday.

Two days later came the bludgeoning in Selma of a white minister, James Reeb. He was targeted because he had the audacity to believe that black citizens had the right to vote. Reverend Reeb subsequently died of his injuries.

Congress and the White House had seen enough. President Lyndon Johnson demanded that the attorney general craft a voting rights bill with teeth. The result was the Voting Rights Act of 1965, the VRA.

The VRA passed with overwhelming majorities in the House of Representatives (328–74) and the Senate (79–18). Johnson signed the bill into law on August 6, 1965. This was almost a year after the president signed into law the landmark Civil Rights Act of 1964, which outlawed discrimination on the job front and in public places (such as in restaurants and on buses and trains) solely because of a person's race, color, sex, religion, or because of where a person was born.

These acts were passed at a time when Democrats had a supermajority in both the House of Representatives and the Senate, though many Republicans supported the acts, too. The majority of opponents came from states that were members of the old Confederacy. Based on federal rights that extended to all, the Civil Rights Act of 1964 outlawed many of the discriminatory practices buttressed by the claim of states' rights, which extended protections and opportunities only to those favored by state law.

And like its sister act in 1964, the 1965 VRA was truly landmark. Rather than waiting for locales to violate voting rights and for people to make formal complaints, the VRA put the responsibility for obeying the Constitution onto state and local governments. The Voting Rights Act, as Michael Waldman so aptly put it in *The Fight to Vote*, "thrust the federal government into the role of supervising voting in large parts of the country to protect African Americans' right to vote, a duty it had not assumed since Reconstruction."

The VRA identified places that had a long, documented history of racial discrimination in voting. Its Section 5 required that the DOJ or the federal court in Washington, DC, approve *any* change to the voting laws or requirements that those districts wanted to make. This was known as "preclearance."

Alabama civil rights attorney Hank Sanders recognized the revolutionary, transformative impact that the preclearance provision could have. Said Sanders: Section 5 of the VRA "can complete something this country started 200 years ago. That something is not complete, it is called Democracy."

But would it hold?

KEY COMPONENTS OF THE VOTING RIGHTS ACT OF 1965

SECTION 2 prohibited impediments created to keep people from voting because of their race or color.

SECTION 3 opened the door to the appointment of federal examiners to oversee voter registration in places where voting rights were violated.

SECTION 4 authorized the federal government to intervene in elections in states and political subdivisions (such as cities and counties) where discrimination was flagrant. Those states and political subdivisions would be determined based on a formula laid out in 4(b). It would apply to places where the US attorney general found that a literacy test, for example, had been in use on November 1, 1964, and where on November 1, 1964, less than 50 percent of eligible voters were registered or if in the presidential election of 1964 less than 50 percent of eligible voters cast a ballot.

When the math was done, authorities determined that the places that needed to be watched were six states of the old Confederacy (Alabama, Georgia, Louisiana, Mississippi, South Carolina, and Virginia) and 39 counties of another state: North Carolina (which has a total of 100 counties).

The covered jurisdictions would be subject to section 5 of the Voting Rights Act of 1965. Section 4 also had a bail-out provision: places could be released from federal scrutiny if, after five years, they proved that they had not engaged in any dirty tricks when it came to voting and voting registration.

SECTION 5 stated that jurisdictions covered in section 4 were forbidden to make changes to voting procedures without "preclearance," that is, without permission from the Department of Justice or the US District Court for the District of Columbia.

(Note that US federal court is structured into three levels. The district courts are the lowest level and are where most federal cases originate. The circuit courts are the intermediate level. The US Supreme Court is the highest level of federal court. Cases often move between levels as verdicts are issued and lawyers appeal decisions or judges determine that a case is outside of their jurisdiction.)

Supreme Court justice Earl Warren maintained that the Voting Rights Act's purpose was to protect against both obvious and subtle attacks on citizens' voting rights.

6

THE WAR ON THE VRA

THE POTENTIAL FOR AN ACTUAL THRIVING, VIABLE
democracy that the Voting Rights Act represented met with a
backlash that gained momentum and velocity in decades to come.

In 1966, a year after the VRA became law, South Carolina
challenged its constitutionality in *South Carolina v. Katzenbach*. The
Palmetto State argued that the VRA violated the state's sovereignty and ability to carry out its own elections. South Carolina
did not, however, prevail.

On March 7, 1966—the first anniversary of Bloody Sunday—in
an 8–1 decision, the US Supreme Court, with Earl Warren as chief
justice, reaffirmed both the *constitutionality* and the *need* for the VRA.

When South Carolina's challenge failed, Mississippi and Virginia took up the battle.

These states acknowledged that disenfranchisement via literacy tests, understanding clauses, and the poll tax was now illegal.
But the two states merely sought to make minor changes to aid

the efficiency of elections. Certainly, those mere tweaks did not require the federal government's okay.

Operating under this assumption, Virginia changed the way it handled voters who were illiterate. Prior to the VRA, there were helpers at the polls for such people. After the VRA, Virginia changed the rules so that voters would have to write in the candidates whose names were not printed on the ballot. In the 1966 state election, those who were illiterate tried to use labels and stickers to indicate their preference only to have those votes discarded according to the new rule requiring the names be handwritten.

Tying the ability to read and write with the vote was no accident. After the 1954 *Brown* decision, Virginia led the effort to make the Supreme Court decision to end segregation in the public schools unenforceable. Lawmakers shut down school districts throughout the state, funneled tax dollars into all-white private academies for white children, and left black children high and dry. This went on for years. Then, after depriving black people of education, the state changed its laws so that those who were illiterate would not be able to vote.

> "The Voting Rights Act was designed by Congress to banish the blight of racial discrimination in voting, which has infected the electoral process in parts of our country for nearly a century. The Act creates stringent new remedies for voting discrimination where it persists on a pervasive scale, and, in addition, the statute strengthens existing remedies for pockets of voting discrimination elsewhere in the country."
>
> —Chief Justice Earl Warren in the 1966
> *South Carolina v. Katzenbach* decision

Mississippi's alterations in voting were equally subtle in their discrimination. After *Brown* and the VRA, positions such as school superintendent suddenly became *appointed* rather than *elected* offices. And whereas county supervisors had once been voted on within their respective, defined districts, now they would be installed via at-large elections, which allows all eligible voters to cast ballots for candidates not in their districts who are running for, say, city council. At-large voting is particularly insidious in areas where black Americans are a sizable part but not a majority of the population.

It works like this: In the original confined districts, black Americans' numbers were large enough to carry enormous electoral weight. Yet literacy tests, poll taxes, and Election Day terror had nullified that power and reduced black voter registration to the single digits. So, there was little possibility of a black candidate—or a white candidate attuned to the black community's concerns— winning an election. After the Voting Rights Act, however, those districts could easily produce progressive elected officials. So Mississippi opted to dilute the black vote among a sea of whites by erasing the district boundaries and requiring candidates to run and succeed in a much wider geographical (and demographic) area. These supposedly race-neutral changes, one Mississippi legislator candidly admitted, would "preserve our way of doing business."

Chief Justice Earl Warren pushed back hard in *Allen v. State Board of Elections* (1969), a consolidation of lawsuits against those voting-related tweaks cooked up by Virginia and Mississippi. When he delivered the majority opinion in the 7–2 decision in March 1969, Warren said that the changes the states had made *were not* beyond the scope of the VRA. Voting is not just the act itself, Warren chided. He reminded the recalcitrant states that the VRA maintained that voting includes "all action necessary to make a vote effective." Then, to ensure that the range of activities subject to the VRA was clear, he insisted that the Voting Rights Act "was aimed at the subtle, as well as the obvious, state regulations which have the effect of denying citizens their right to vote because of race."

For years, states continued to chafe against the VRA. Then in 2013 came the US Supreme Court's ruling in *Shelby County v. Holder.* Here, "Shelby" was a county in Alabama and "Holder" was Eric Holder, the nation's first black US attorney general.

In its 5–4 *Shelby* decision, the High Court eviscerated the VRA.

Many of the arguments that Chief Justice John Roberts made matched those put forth for decades by VRA opponents.

ARGUMENT #1:
The federal government had overstepped its authority. A cornerstone for this charge was Justice Hugo Black's lone dissent in the 1966 *South Carolina v. Katzenbach* case. Black took aim at the preclearance provision. He argued that it "so distorts our constitutional structure of government as to render any distinction drawn in the Constitution between state and federal power almost meaningless."

ARGUMENT #2:
The VRA had been a success and so was no longer needed. Yes, the VRA had been a success. "In Mississippi, black registration went from less than 10 percent in 1964 to almost 60 percent in 1968; in Alabama, the figure rose from 24 percent to 57 percent,"

stated Alexander Keyssar in *The Right to Vote*. "In the region as a whole, roughly a million new voters were registered within a few years after the bill became law, bringing African-American registration to a record 62 percent." But remember: the VRA was effective precisely because it was a robust, muscular law.

ARGUMENT #3:
The VRA picked on the South. In 1970, Senator Strom Thurmond of South Carolina, one of the most powerful members of Congress, insisted that the VRA was "nothing more than a device created to inflict political punishment upon one section of the country."

Such thinking totally ignored decades of Election Day terror, literacy tests, poll taxes, and white primaries. It failed to explain the fact that as late as World War II, fewer than 1 percent of age-eligible blacks were registered to vote in South Carolina. It also ignored stats like this: when Thurmond uttered those infamous words in 1970, only "28 percent of blacks were registered in Thurmond's home of Edgefield County, compared with 96 percent of whites," Ari Berman pointed out in his book *Give Us the Ballot*.

ARGUMENT #4:
A pernicious lie, one that hovered like a storm cloud over the VRA and became darker and more threatening as black political power grew: Voter Fraud.

In the years following the passage of the VRA, key segments in the criminal justice and political system insisted that the real voting violators were not the states but black people. Alabama civil rights attorney Hank Sanders had witnessed this vicious scenario play out. Whenever blacks won political office or started to assert their voting rights, he remarked, the prosecutor's office would launch an extensive investigation. This move had but one purpose: intimidation. "Every time people start investigating you," he explained, "you start drawing back and decide no matter how right you are to leave that alone," because if you don't, the criminal justice system will rip you apart for simply exercising your voting rights. People in Pickens County, Alabama, learned that all too well after county elections in 1978.

Julia Wilder, a black woman who was president of the Pickens County Voters League and an officer of the Southern Christian Leadership Conference (SCLC), had been hard at work to make the Voting Rights Act viable in rural Alabama. By the late 1970s, no black American had ever been elected to county office in Pickens, a county that was 42 percent black.

Joining Wilder, then in her sixties, was Maggie Bozeman, a black woman and president of the local NAACP. For the 1978 county elections, Wilder and Bozeman collected absentee ballots from more than three dozen elderly black people, had those forms certified as valid by a notary, then sent them to the Board of Elections.

Enter Sophie Spann.

On Election Day 1978, this black woman went down to the local grocery store to cast her vote but was turned away. An election official told Sophie Spann that she had already voted.

Absentee.

That set off an investigation by the Pickens County district attorney followed by a tumultuous, haphazard trial that was so riddled with holes and contradictions that the appeals court labeled the key witnesses' testimony "confusing," "conflicting," and an indecipherable "hodgepodge."

Of the original and alleged thirteen "victims," the only one who remained steadfast in insisting that her vote was stolen was Sophie Spann, who just happened, wrote one journalist, to have "reared the sheriff's deputy and son-in-law" and who was brought lunch by the sheriff personally before she took the stand. Based on Spann's testimony alone, Julia Wilder and Maggie Bozeman were found guilty by an all-white jury. The verdict was upheld by the appeals court.

In January 1982, Bozeman, then fifty-one, received a four-year prison sentence.

Wilder, sixty-nine, got hit with the maximum, five years. "The sentences are believed to be the stiffest ever given in an Alabama voting fraud case," reported the *Washington Post*.

The two activists deemed troublemakers by the white power structure had pushed for and won better wages for sanitation workers and to have roads paved in black neighborhoods. And their commitment to black voting rights was unshakable. For example, if it meant giving someone her last fifty cents "to get to the polls," that's what Wilder was going to do. If it meant teaching a civics lesson to those who had been beaten down for so long that they didn't think their vote mattered, she had no problem with that, either.

For many in the black community, the district attorney going after Bozeman and Wilder was nothing but retribution "for trying to make democracy work." The sheriff disagreed vigorously. There was no need for what Wilder and Bozeman did. Blacks had it good in Pickens County. "We have a policy of not beating 'em," he bragged. "We treat 'em right. We don't run over 'em just because they are black."

In the end, a measure of mercy prevailed for Wilder and Bozeman—that is, after protests on their behalf. "The women spent less than two weeks at an Alabama prison before they were transferred to special work release assignments and permitted to live in a private home in heavily black-populated Macon County, some 200 miles from their home," reported the United Press International (UPI) news agency on November 10, 1982. "Mrs. Bozeman taught classes at a mental health center in the Tuskegee work release program and will teach at a school in Sumter County, adjacent to her home county, while she is on parole. Mrs. Wilder, a quiet, frail woman, worked at a senior citizens center in her work release assignment."

Three years after Wilder and Bozeman began serving their sentences, in 1985, then–US attorney for the Southern District of Alabama Jefferson Beauregard Sessions III slapped three civil rights workers with a twenty-nine-count indictment for forging or changing and then mailing bogus absentee ballots. His primary target was Albert Turner Sr., a former aide to Martin Luther King Jr.

Albert Turner Sr. entered the voting rights battle in the early 1960s after he, a college-educated man, failed Alabama's literacy test. Infuriated, Turner threw himself into grassroots organizing. He was knee-deep in the battles in Selma. He formed the Perry County Civic League to register more black men and women to vote and change what democracy looked like in Alabama.

Working with his wife, Evelyn, and colleague Stephen Hogue, Turner noticed that despite the VRA, and despite the large number of black people in Alabama's Black Belt counties (so-called because of the region's rich, dark soil), white people consistently won *every* election. As Turner dug deeper, he learned that the difference was the sheer volume of absentee ballots from whites who were landowners in Perry, Lowndes, and other counties but lived in Birmingham, Chicago, and elsewhere. Election officials in the Black Belt, including in Perry County (60 percent black) actively encouraged these white people to use the absentee ballots to keep political power in white hands.

The absentee ballot was not something that blacks used extensively. And Perry County was prime for it.

Almost one-third of Perry County's black adults worked in another county. What's more, 15 percent of its black residents were over sixty-five years old. In short, 48 percent of the black vote was already in jeopardy because of employment obligations and a lack of mobility. And there was this: the polls were open for only four hours in the afternoon on Election Day. The absentee ballot would be a godsend for black people who could not vote because of their work schedule, distance to the polls, or limited mobility during that narrow four-hour window.

Turner went to the Alabama attorney general's office for training sessions and then began to apply that knowledge in Perry and surrounding counties. Not surprisingly, Election Day 1982 brought a very different result. Blacks won positions on the school boards and county commissions.

The Perry County district attorney cried foul! He was convinced that Turner and company had committed fraud. The DA quickly informed US attorney Jeff Sessions, who hated the VRA, considering it a meddling piece of legislation.

When the next primary rolled around in 1984, Sessions

had the FBI tail the Turners and Stephen Hogue. After the trio mailed hundreds of absentee ballots they had collected, the agents seized the ballots, and, after picking through them, believed they had identified seventy-five that had been tampered with. Sessions then identified the victims of the alleged voter fraud, moved them south to Mobile, and interviewed them there.

Note that in his investigations, Sessions targeted only counties where blacks had won office. He deliberately ignored districts that maintained white political control via absentee ballots and summarily dismissed evidence of irregularities in those votes as not being "credible."

And so in Perry County, he rounded up some twenty elderly black people and had state troopers drive them 160 miles away, to a predominately white area, to be fingerprinted, photographed, and grilled before a grand jury. It was a terrifying experience.

For Reverend O. C. Dobynes it was "the most degrading thing." And he was clear about the point of all that drama: "To me, it was just simply saying, 'We are going to scare you into saying what we want you to say.'"

It worked.

Fannie Mae Williams told the grand jury that this was her "first and last" time voting using an absentee ballot.

Two others were even more emphatic: they "were done with voting," wrote Emily Bazelon in her 2017 *New York Times Magazine* piece "The Voter Fraud Case Jeff Sessions Lost and Can't Escape."

"Ninety-two-year-old Willie Bright was so frightened of 'the law' that he wouldn't even admit he'd voted," reported Ari Berman in a 2016 piece for *The Nation* magazine, "Jeff Sessions,

Trump's Pick for Attorney General, Is a Fierce Opponent of Civil Rights."

In the end, after a grand jury indictment, then a trial, Albert Turner, Evelyn Turner, and Stephen Hogue were found not guilty of *any* wrongdoing. There had been no voter fraud.

That trial, like Bozeman and Wilder's, signaled how to use "the criminal processes . . . to slow down the development of progressive black leadership." And it was yet another example of marshaling the forces of legal intimidation to trigger communal memories of brutality, Jim Crow, and disenfranchisement. Even years after her ordeal with Jeff Sessions, Evelyn Turner declared, "I'll never forget, as long as I stay black."

Presidential candidate Al Gore's supporters protest after the Supreme Court ruling that granted George W. Bush the win in 2000.

7

A "JUDICIAL COUP D'ÉTAT"

ALONG WITH THE CRIES THAT THE FEDERAL GOV-
ernment had overstepped its authority, that the VRA had been a
success and so was no longer needed, that it picked on the South,
and that there was rampant voter fraud afoot, haters of the VRA
had on their side the ease with which the US Supreme Court
overturned a federal election.

This happened in 2000 when the presidency hung by a chad.

The face-off was between Republican George W. Bush, son of
the forty-first US president, George Herbert Walker Bush, and
Democratic vice president Al Gore.

On the night of November 7, 2000, forty-nine states had tallied their ballots. Bush and Gore were in a virtual tie as the world
waited for the count from Florida. Whoever won its twenty-five
Electoral College votes would become the forty-third US
president.

Florida was a festering election cesspool—as racially backward as it was bureaucratically inept. Secretary of State Katherine Harris had used faulty data to purge approximately twenty thousand names, mostly of blacks and Latinos, from the voter rolls. In polling stations in Jacksonville's black neighborhoods, police officers stationed themselves conspicuously around the buildings and at entry points as if this were Mississippi in the 1950s all over again. In other cases, voters who knew they were registered learned on Election Day that their names were nowhere to be found on the registrar's list. Poll workers could not get in touch with election officials to do any kind of verification because the phone lines were jammed. There was a more effective method of verification using laptop computers, but those were placed in predominately white, Republican precincts.

There were also a limited number of working voting machines in polling stations that had sizable populations of people of color.

In some areas, none of the machines tallied even one vote for a presidential candidate. Not one.

And then there were the hanging chads.

Some voting machines punched a hole next to a candidate's name, others made a dent, while others left the little circular piece of paper dangling. The debris from a punched hole is known as a chad, and the irregularity of these ballot markings led to arguments over just what was considered a marked ballot.

The voting machines, unable to get an accurate count—not least because of the ballots with imperfect chad punches—were blamed. Gore therefore requested a hand recount. And that's when the momentum swung, as Bush's margin of victory began to shrink rapidly, from 1,784 votes to 327, then to 154.

It was at this nail-biting moment that the US Supreme Court stepped in, overruling Florida's highest court, and ordered that the recount stop. Five conservative justices, who often denounced what they called an activist judiciary and federal overreach in general, now ruled that Florida did not have the right to count the ballots in the election held in its own state. In fact, no entity could tally those votes. The recount violated the Fourteenth Amendment's equal protection clause, the justices contended, because the process was for those counties with numerous electoral failures and, therefore, some people, somehow, somewhere (that would be in those counties where the polling machines actually worked) weren't going to have their votes counted again.

The argument defied logic. That is, until it became clear that this was about one thing and one thing alone: putting Republican George W. Bush in the White House. Before Gore called for a recount, Secretary of State Katherine Harris had certified Bush the winner of the Florida's twenty-five electoral votes. The US Supreme Court let that stand.

A "judicial coup d'état."
—Attorney Vincent Bugliosi on the Supreme Court's decision in his book *The Betrayal of America: How the Supreme Court Undermined the Constitution and Chose Our President*

That 2000 presidential election set the stage for a new component that Justice John Roberts would use to essentially kill the Voting Rights Act. Over time, more and more members of

the US Supreme Court had begun to openly question the constitutionality of preclearance.

The election, and particularly how it was won, had driven
home how racially polarized and divided the electorate was.
George W. Bush, however, didn't believe the situation was
hopeless.

While only 9 percent of black Americans voted for him,
35 percent of Latinos had given him the thumbs-up. His strate-
gist, therefore, argued that the Republicans could broaden their
appeal to people of color and thus avert the demographic apoca-
lypse that awaited a party that was nearly 90 percent white. In
addition to immigration reform, one of his key strategies was to
have full White House and bipartisan support for the 2006 reauthorization of the Voting Rights Act.

Aided by a phalanx of civil rights organizations, Congress
amassed and reviewed reams of research and data on discrimination in voting, and with a 390–33 vote in the House of Representatives (on July 13, 2006) and a 98–0 vote in the Senate (on
July 20, 2006), reauthorized the Voting Rights Act for another
twenty-five years. Many of the VRA's original or subsequent features still remained, including targeting, as Alexander Keyssar
explained in *The Right To Vote*, "the same states and counties for
special coverage, while preserving both Section 5 preclearance
requirement and the language assistance provisions," which had
arisen during the 1982 reauthorization hearings to acknowledge
the documented attempts to disenfranchise Latinos.

President George W. Bush signed the VRA Extension Act
into law on July 27, 2006.

Within days, a small, recently formed municipality in Texas

sued the Department of Justice. It claimed that because it did not have some sordid history of racial discrimination, it should not have to abide by the preclearance statute just because it was located in the Lone Star State. In short: while Texas had a history of discrimination, it did not. This municipality was the Northwest Austin Municipal Utility District Number One (NAMUDNO). The lawsuit was *NAMUDNO v. Holder.*

The lawsuit also depicted the Voting Rights Act as a dinosaur. As Keyssar explained, the suit charged that "racial discrimination was no longer the problem it had been in 1965 and that Section 5 imposed unfair and unnecessary burdens on the jurisdictions that it covered."

The court wasn't quite ready to go that far. At least not yet. While allowing the Voting Rights Act to stay in place for now, key members of the court, especially Chief Justice John Roberts, signaled discontent with what they saw as a stagnant VRA, which failed to take into account that Jim Crow was dead and America had moved on. This was not 1899, after all, or even 1969.

Long an opponent of the Voting Rights Act, Roberts had clerked under Justice William Rehnquist, whose initial foray into voting rights prior to his ascent to the Supreme Court included a project to purge as many people of color as possible from voting rolls in Phoenix, Arizona. Rehnquist's appointment to the bench only strengthened his opposition. In one case, the US Supreme Court had overturned a multiyear scheme in Rome, Georgia, that, without gaining preclearance approval, repeatedly annexed white areas to the city to reduce the electoral potential of black voters. Rehnquist was unfazed by the city's (illegal) actions and instead depicted the VRA as simply black peoples' way to get revenge on the heirs of slaveholders. "The enforcement provisions of the Civil War Amendments [Fourteenth and Fifteenth]," he wrote in his dissent, "were not premised on the notion that Congress could empower a later generation of blacks to 'get even' for wrongs inflicted on their forebears."

This was the man who served as an ideological light for John Roberts. "Rehnquist reinforced John's preexisting philosophies," observed a colleague clerking for another justice. "John was not a believer in the courts giving rights to minorities and the downtrodden. That was the basic Rehnquist philosophy."

The framing of the Rehnquist-Roberts philosophy is key. Note that the word used is "giving" instead of simply recognizing that people of color have rights. Thus Roberts's subsequent stint in President Ronald Reagan's Civil Rights Division of the Department of Justice honed his antipathy to the VRA. "John seemed like he always had it in for the Voting Rights Act," remembered J. Gerald Hebert, one of the chief litigators for the DOJ on voting. "I remember him being a zealot when it came to having fundamental suspicions about the Voting Rights Act's utility."

Adding to Roberts's disdain was the way Congress, during its 1982 reauthorization of the Voting Rights Act, wiped away an earlier court ruling that required the DOJ to prove that there was a deliberate intent to discriminate in order for there to be a VRA violation. That decision said that prima facie evidence of discrimination was not enough, even when staring right at a city like Mobile, Alabama, which was 35 percent black and had never—even after the VRA—elected any black person as a city commissioner. Instead, the court ruled that the DOJ would have to prove that officials in Mobile deliberately crafted the voting requirements to dilute the electoral strength of its black population. Intent, of course, was a nearly impossible threshold of proof, requiring racially explicit memos or taped conversations.

The 1982 reauthorization of the VRA removed Roberts's beloved "intent to discriminate" standard, which led him to predict, insist even, that the Voting Rights Act would require election results ruled by quotas and affirmative action. But as Ari Berman noted, "In the seven southern states originally covered by the VRA . . . blacks made up 25 percent of the population but held only 5 percent of elected seats." Roberts's fears were just that, fears. "In a lot of cases . . . there were no blacks elected," said civil rights lawyer Armand Derfner. "We were trying to get from none to some." Roberts didn't see the virtual shutout in many municipalities and counties; instead he focused on districts such as Atlanta and Houston, which had elected blacks and Latinos, and, therefore, to him it was unfair that Georgia and Texas remained under the preclearance provisions.

So, when *NAMUDNO v. Holder* was decided in 2009, years of doubt about the Voting Rights Act, years of questioning whether racism existed anymore, came to a boil. "Since 1982," Roberts wrote in his decision, "only 17 jurisdictions—out of the more than 12,000 covered political subdivisions—have successfully bailed out of the Act." That only seventeen had been able to prove they no longer discriminated against their minority populations' voting rights and thus no longer needed federal oversight seemed absurd to Roberts. He, of course, did not reckon with the fact that places in Georgia and Alabama such as Pickens County,

Perry County, and Rome had repeatedly tried to disenfranchise American citizens despite the Fifteenth Amendment, and that is the reason only seventeen jurisdictions had been released from scrutiny in more than four decades. Instead, came the court's warning shot: seventeen was not enough. "It is unlikely that Congress intended the provision to have such limited effect."

Thus, when the commissioners in Shelby County, Alabama, challenged the Voting Rights Act by outright defying it, the US Supreme Court was already primed and just waiting for a test case.

Calera City, Alabama, had a city council that included one black councilman. His district was 65 percent black, in a city that was over 30 percent black. Then the commissioners in Shelby County began annexing land surrounding Calera City, and with each annexation they began to redraw the electoral districts, so much so that the black councilman's district population shrank from 65 percent black to 29 percent. Running now in a predominately white district, where more than three-fourths of the electorate voted against Barack Obama, the lone black councilman lost the next election.

This was not the first time that the Supreme Court had dealt with the redrawing of a city's boundaries designed to dilute the voting strength of a town's black population. In the late 1950s, black people in Tuskegee, Alabama, had begun, against all odds, to amass some semblance of voting strength. The state legislature quickly countered by annexing plot after plot of land surrounding Tuskegee until the town's perfectly symmetrical square boundaries had been horribly disfigured into a twenty-eight-sided blob. This is what it took to remove all but four or five of the four hundred voting-age eligible black people from the city and ensure that no white voter was excluded. Alabama argued that it had the authority to change its city boundaries whenever and however it chose and it didn't need a reason.

Justice William O. Douglas explained how mistaken Alabama truly was. He systematically laid out how the state, despite multiple queries, could come up with no viable reason for its actions. There was only one way to explain why four hundred black voters became a mere four or five, to explain why a perfectly logical city boundary devolved into one with twenty-eight sides, to explain why, even with all those changes, Tuskegee did not lose one white voter. Alabama had set out to strip black people of their right to vote. And that, Douglas insisted, violated the Fifteenth Amendment.

Fifty-three years later, Chief Justice John Roberts looked directly at a similar situation where county commissioners in Alabama had annexed plot after plot, redrawn boundaries, diluted the voting strength of black voters, and, this time, done so in violation of the Voting Rights Act. Unlike before, however, the Supreme Court, in a 5–4, decision, ignored all the evidence and drew instead upon the arguments hurled against the VRA since 1966. Refrains about states' rights, black electoral success, regional discrimination, the end of racism, and the seeming calcification of the VRA became the key elements in the decision penned by Chief Justice Roberts in *Shelby County v. Holder.*

The court decided that the VRA was unfair because it singled out and punished the South (which obviously meant whites in the South), unfair because the 2006 reauthorization included the same states and counties as in the original bill, unfair because blacks had won multiple elections and were voting in record numbers, and unfair because the racism of the past, which had led to the creation of the VRA, obviously no longer determined access to the polls. The *Shelby County v. Holder* decision gutted Section 4 of the Voting Rights Act, which determined which locales came under federal oversight. With that, GOP-led states asserted that it was actually voter fraud, not voter suppression, that required the full machinery of government to eradicate.

As a result, 2016 was the first federal election in fifty years held without the protection of the Voting Rights Act.

An election in which millions of votes vanished into thin air.

★ PART TWO ★

VOTER ID

Anthony Settles (left) meets with his attorney. Settles was denied the right to vote because the last name on his photo ID didn't match the name on his birth certificate.

8

"A CITIZEN NO MORE"

FLOYD CARRIER WAS A PROUD KOREAN WAR VETERAN.

He was also black and living near Beaumont, Texas. And that put his voting rights in the state's crosshairs.

In 2012, when this senior citizen went to his local polling place to vote, he wasn't allowed to do so. He was told that his Veterans Administration card—an acceptable form of ID for decades—was no longer valid. To vote he had to have a government-issued *photo* ID. The man was devastated: "I wasn't a citizen no more," he told a journalist.

Other Americans also realized that they, too, had just crossed into the twilight zone of American-lite: a citizen without full citizenship rights.

Another black man, Anthony Settles of Houston, found himself blocked from the ballot because when he was a teen growing up in the DC area his mother changed his last name to that of the man she married. In order for Settles to obtain a photo ID in the name he was applying under—the name he had been using for more than half a century—it had to be a match with the name on his birth certificate. The only fix was to produce the official document bearing proof of his name change when he was a teen. It was a "bureaucratic nightmare," the retired engineer told a reporter in 2016. And Settles was not confused about Texas's strict voter ID law: "The intent of this law is to suppress the vote. I feel like I am not wanted in this state."

Dear Gov. Abbott,
Despite the fact I am an American citizen, I want you to know that I have not been able to vote in any election since Texas passed its voter ID law in 2013. My constitutional rights have been stripped from me.

I am contacting you because, as a disabled person, I thought you would understand my situation. I, too, am a person with a disability. I am in a wheelchair. Because of my severe cerebral palsy, I can't talk, I can't drive and I don't have a driver's license.

Still, I earned a college degree in journalism from the University of North Texas in 2005.

In the past, I had no problem voting. All I had to do was present my voter card at the polls after I had registered to vote.

After the new law passed, it required a photo ID for voting. My most recent one expired in 2006. To obtain a new identity card, I have to rely on people to take me to a Texas Department of Public Safety office and provide documentation. . . .

The new ID requirement of forcing a person to show a utility bill to get an ID has created a huge obstacle in obtaining the identification card for voters with disabilities. I don't have a utility bill to show anyone. I don't have a bank account.

—from a July 2017 open letter to Texas governor Greg Abbott, from Jeremiah "Jay" Prophet, a white writer. Governor Abbott was paralyzed below the waist after an accident when in his twenties.

When it came to throwing up new barriers to voting, Texas was not alone.

Almost thirteen hundred miles away, Sean Reynolds, a Navy veteran who had returned home in 2015 after serving in Iraq and Afghanistan, went to the polls only to learn that his valid Illinois driver's license was a no-go in his new home state, Wisconsin.

Reynolds's fifty-hour work week was hard enough. Getting time off to go to the local Department of Motor Vehicles (DMV) to secure a new license wasn't easy. On top of that, Republican governor Scott Walker had shortened the operating hours or removed many of the DMVs in the Democratic stronghold of Milwaukee—where 70 percent of the state's black population lived.

And in Madison where Sean Reynolds lived. "Coming home" from a war zone, he said, "and being denied the right to vote because I didn't have a specific driver's license" was "very frustrating."

Americans in Iowa, Indiana, and Pennsylvania could relate. In the twenty-first century, the geography of voter suppression had clearly changed. Whereas it was once primarily a phenomenon of the Jim Crow South, by 2017 voter suppression, a Republican-fueled monstrosity, had gripped thirty-three states and cast a pall over more than half the American voting-age population.

The new disenfranchising beast was born in Florida during the controversial 2000 presidential election.

Florida secretary of state Katherine Harris was one of George W. Bush's campaign co-chairs, and she used her authority to undermine recount efforts in Florida.

FLORIDA FIASCO, MISSOURI MADNESS, HOOSIER STATE HORRORS, AND GEORGIA NOT SO PEACHY KEEN

HANGING CHADS, BROKEN MACHINES, POLICE HOVER-
ing around the polls, and purged voter rolls had "put great stress
on the public's faith in electoral integrity," wrote legal scholar
Richard L. Hasen of the 2000 election in his book *The Voting Wars.*

With the electoral chaos in Florida and the inability to get an
accurate tally, it soon began to dawn on many Americans that
democracy in the United States was not the well-oiled machine it
purported to be. Said Hasen: it was "a wake-up call."

To regain the nation's trust, a bipartisan commission, led by
former presidents Jimmy Carter and Gerald Ford, set out to identify the deficiencies in the election process and make solid recommendations to address the weaknesses. But the carefully laid-out

process and, more important, the overall goal, had already been hijacked in Missouri.

Just as in Florida, Election Day 2000 in St. Louis was a "chaotic mess," wrote Lorraine C. Minnite in her book *The Myth of Voter Fraud*. The chaos stemmed from the fact that the St. Louis City Board of Elections had illegally purged some fifty-thousand names from the voter rolls in key Democratic precincts. What's more, it failed, as the law required, to notify the people it had disenfranchised.

Not surprisingly, when those voters showed up to cast their ballots, they were dumbfounded to discover that they were no longer registered to vote.

Besieged precinct workers couldn't get through on the jammed phone lines to check or double-check much of anything. They opted to send frustrated would-be voters downtown to the Board of Elections office to resolve the issue.

Poor record keeping and ill-prepared and ill-informed officials meant that hours and hours passed away as the clock on Election Day wound down. "By early evening, the lobby [at the Board of Elections] was shoulder to shoulder with people who wanted to vote," said a news report.

As closing time at the polls loomed, Democrats filed for an injunction to keep the doors open for a few more hours to accommodate voters who had been caught in the Board of Election's illegal purge and runaround. A local judge agreed and ordered the polls to stay open for three additional hours, until 10 p.m.

But moments later, Republicans pleaded with a higher court

to close the polls at the agreed-upon time. Missouri's senator Christopher "Kit" Bond charged that the lower court's ruling allowing those three additional hours "represents the biggest fraud on the voters in this state and nation that we have ever seen."

Within forty-five minutes, the lower court's ruling was overturned. The doors slammed shut on crowds waiting to cast their ballots.

But it would get worse.

Missouri Republicans twisted a clear case of election board wrongdoing into a torrent of accusations against the black residents in St. Louis and the Democrats.

Missouri secretary of state Matt Blunt called the effort to keep the polls open a "conspiracy to create bedlam so that election fraud could be perpetrated." It was not. It was, instead, an illegal purge of 49,589 eligible voters by the Board of Elections. It was also sloppy record keeping and bureaucratic malfeasance. But, for the GOP, that was not the point. Rather, the Republicans used this bungled election to walk away with several key lessons.

Lesson #1: demographics was not destiny. The voting-age population was becoming increasingly black, Latino, and Asian. In 1992, for example, nonwhite voters made up 13 percent of the electorate; by 2012 they made up 28 percent, and that growing share of the electorate tilted heavily toward the Democrats. In the *Bush v. Gore* 2000 presidential election, 90 percent of black, 62 percent of Latino, and 55 percent of Asian voters cast their ballots for Al Gore. The big takeaway for the GOP was the need to block members of those groups from the polls by virtually any means necessary.

Lesson #2: the importance of controlling the electoral machinery that decided the rules for voting, the conditions upon which those votes would be cast, and whose vote counted and whose did not. Florida secretary of state Katherine Harris proved this point beyond all doubt.

A delegate at the Republican National Convention and one of George W. Bush's campaign co-chairs, Harris used her authority and power to undermine the recount. And she had the full support of George W. Bush's brother, Florida governor Jeb Bush, who surreptitiously sent in fixer Mac Stipanovich to keep the secretary of state focused on the job at hand. Knowing that his presence would be, as he himself later said, "provocative," Stipanovich devised ingenious ways to get in and out of the capitol building without the media seeing him.

The key was to override the state's law that identified "intent of the voter" as the "gold standard" for a manual recount in Florida.

Was the hanging chad or indentation clear on the ballot but unreadable by the machine?

Had the voter written in the preferred candidate's name instead of marking the oval, etc.?

When some of the counties began their manual tabulation of a representative sample of the ballots, they used the "gold standard" to guide their process.

Suddenly, Gore was gaining ground fast, which meant this could trigger a full-blown recount. All of a sudden, the criterion for a county to have a recount became stricter.

The voting machines had to be completely broken, not simply malfunctioning, the secretary of state ruled. Then Harris

tried to short-circuit the process further by moving up the dead-
line date for when the manual count had to be completed, which
was actually well before two of the major counties, including
Miami-Dade, "had even decided whether to recount, and before
Broward had finished." Harris simply "sowed confusion." In
one egregious case, she altered the rules to determine which absentee ballots were valid and which were not, and the most salient
feature in that change was the political tilt of the county: Republican-
leaning counties received a much more expansive set of parameters
and were advised that they could count overseas ballots that were
completed—and not necessarily postmarked—on Election Day.
Democratic counties, however, had been handed the opposite
advice, which diminished greatly the number of eligible ballots.
As a result, George W. Bush, although losing the nationwide
popular vote, carried Florida by 537 votes, won the Electoral College, and, with a very key assist by the US Supreme Court,
became the forty-third president of the United States.

Lesson #3: Lie. Lie often, loudly, boldly, unashamedly, and
consistently.

Lie until it drowns out the truth.

Lie until no amount of evidence could prove otherwise.

Lie until there was no other reigning narrative.

Just lie.

Senator Bond learned this lesson well. He claimed that scores
of Democrats were using the names of dead people and dogs
to vote repeatedly. He insisted that others were basically stuffing
the ballot box by creating fictitious addresses where there were
only vacant lots. Just as the best lies hold a kernel of truth,
Bond chose well. Some prankster had, indeed, registered a

thirteen-year-old springer spaniel, Ritzy Mekler, to vote. Yet there is no record anywhere of Fido, Rover, Lassie, or even the infamous Ritzy casting a ballot, as Bond claimed.

As for addresses alleged to be empty lots—that lie also collapsed under scrutiny. When the *St. Louis Post-Dispatch* investigated, it found that 82 percent of the suspicious addresses were "wrongly classified by the city assessor's office as vacant" because they "in fact contained legitimate residences." This bureaucratic snafu even "snared" St. Louis's top budget official, Frank Jackson, whose ten-year-old condominium had never, even after a decade, made it off the city's vacant lot register.

Most of the remaining suspicious voters had been flagged because a large number of adults had registered the same address as their respective home. When reporters visited those sites, however, it turned out that, indeed, while these might not be group homes, apartments, or nursing homes, "more than eight people properly lived at the address noted." Other "suspect voters" were mislabeled as fraudulent because of typographical errors or because they had actually moved within the city and did not have to reregister.

And, just as with Ritzy the dog, Bond eventually found a dead person on the voter registration rolls: a former city alderman. But there was no evidence that the deceased or anyone with his name voted in the 2000 election.

By the time every one of Bond's three hundred plus claims was investigated, it was clear that out of 2.3 million voters in Missouri, the four people who committed some type of malfeasance at the polls hardly constituted rampant voter fraud. And it was also obvious that "none of these problems could have been resolved by requiring photo ID at the polls." Yet, from the tattered cloths of bureaucratic snafus, administrative incompetence, and typographical errors, the lie of rampant voter fraud hung there, dangling, as the senator kept fashioning democracy's noose.

In 2001, Missouri's Kit Bond became the senator tasked with guiding a bill through Congress to re-instill the American public's confidence in the electoral system. The nation's concern about the racism and inadequacies that were on full display on Election Day 2000 were real. Bond, however, was determined to keep the fiction of rampant voter fraud front and center.

The result was the 2002 Help America Vote Act (HAVA). Because of the good work of the Carter-Ford Commission, HAVA was filled with all kinds of positive innovations such as an Election Assistance Commission to help states modernize and standardize voting systems. The law also provided a clear mandate to update voting machines and a mechanism to register complaints.

There was also a poison pill, something Kit Bond had insisted on.

In exchange for allowing the replacement of the infamous hanging chad machines, Kit Bond demanded that HAVA have language requiring that people have photo identification in order to vote. Initially, it seemed harmless enough.

The requirement for ID was supposed to be limited to voters who had originally registered by mail. It was also supposed to allow a range of documents by which a citizen could verify his or her identity: documents such as employee IDs, student IDs, paychecks, and driver's licenses. What it actually did, though, was give federal credence, in law, to the lie of rampant voter fraud. Thus, a dangerous false equivalency emerged. There was the hard-core reality of voter suppression in Florida and St. Louis (purged rolls, faulty machines, and more) that had disenfranchised tens of thousands of American citizens. And then there was Kit Bond's fantasy of stuffed ballot boxes. With HAVA, the lie had become the truth.

What made the law even more problematic was that the Carter-Ford Commission had estimated that "as many as 19 million potential voters nationwide did not possess either a driver's license or a state issued photo ID" and those "most likely to be adversely affected . . . were disproportionately young, elderly, poor, and African American." That was key. All that had to happen was for the GOP to reinforce the lie of voter fraud, create the public perception of democracy imperiled, increase the groundswell to "protect the integrity of the ballot box," require exactly the type of identification that blacks, the poor, the young, and the elderly did not have, and, equally important, mask these acts of aggressive voter suppression behind the nobility of being "civic-minded."

From 2005 to 2013, the Republicans did just that. In congressional hearings on strengthening election integrity, Republican attorney Mark "Thor" Hearne became a frequent expert witness on rampant voter fraud. Hearne, who like Kit Bond had opposed St. Louis voters having those extra three hours at the polls, did this as a representative of the American Center for Voting Rights (ACVR).

The ACVR had a bright, shiny webpage with a photo of an array of racially diverse Americans. It had links to "policy

papers" and "data," along with a very impressive bio of its director, Thor Hearne. ACVR seemed substantial enough to be the
major source of information to Congress about massive voting
irregularities throughout the United States. It was, as legal
scholar Hasen pointed out, "the only prominent nongovernmental organization claiming that voter fraud is a major problem, a
problem warranting strict rules such as voter-ID laws."

Yet, the organization's substance and heft was also a lie. As
Hasen revealed in his article "The Fraudulent Fraud Squad,"
the ACVR "was founded just days before its representatives
testified before a congressional committee hearing on election-
administration issues. . . . Consisting of little more than a post-
office box and some staffers who wrote reports and gave helpful
quotes about the pervasive problems of voter fraud to the press,
the group identified Democratic cities as hot spots for voter
fraud, then pushed the line that 'election integrity' required making it harder for people to vote."

Thor Hearne gave it his all. In hearing after hearing, press
conference after press conference, op-ed after op-ed, he filled the
ether with tales of people impersonating someone else to destroy
the integrity of America's elections. As for those supposed "hot
spots" of systemic voter fraud, there were five: each with a black
or at least nonwhite population that made up 32 to 95 percent of
the city's residents:

> Philadelphia, Pennsylvania
> Milwaukee, Wisconsin
> Seattle, Washington
> St. Louis, Missouri/East St. Louis, Illinois
> Cleveland, Ohio

The ACVR served up baseless rumors and false anecdotes dressed as fact. It dished out new, tantalizing, and wholly erroneous reports of the NAACP paying for votes with crack cocaine. The disinformation program was malevolently brilliant and effective.

> "In 2005 Hearne was pushing allegations about voter fraud in St. Louis from 2000 that had been thoroughly debunked in 2002."
> —Richard L. Hasen in *The Voting Wars: From Florida 2000 to the Next Election Meltdown*

Almost as soon as that narrative of voter fraud was out there, gaining traction, providing sound bites for politicians and creating the basis for shaping voter ID legislation, ACVR, along with its PO box and website, went *poof!* So did mention on Hearne's résumé of his role in this scam.

President George W. Bush had also turned the supposed need to protect the integrity of the ballot box from rampant voter fraud into "public policy." In 2002, America's top cop, Attorney General John Ashcroft, a former senator from Missouri, made this a high priority for the Department of Justice and federal prosecutors. They scoured major cities with large people-of-color populations looking for cases to substantiate Kit Bond's, Matt Blunt's, and Thor Hearne's tales of electoral chicanery. They found a few felons who didn't know they couldn't vote yet. They uncovered a handful of permanent residents who misunderstood the laws about voting. That was it. Nevertheless, inordinate pressure from Republican US senators and DOJ officials continued.

Some federal prosecutors dug in and refused to bring charges and give credence to the GOP's voter fraud claims right before the 2006 midterm election because there was little to no evidence of wrongdoing. David Iglesias, the US attorney in New Mexico, for example, saw no reason to file charges in an instance where someone registered a thirteen-year-old boy to vote unbeknownst to him and his parents. For that and similar acts of integrity, Iglesias and seven other federal prosecutors were fired.

"There was nothing that we uncovered that suggested some sort of concerted effort to tilt the election," concluded Richard G. Frohling, the assistant US attorney in Milwaukee, supposedly a "hot spot" of voter fraud. But all this activity, all this searching, gave the illusion of widespread voter fraud that needed to be ferreted out and stopped.

And Indiana stepped into the breach.

Indiana's secretary of state Todd Rokita, a Republican, and Indiana's Republican legislators set out to add a powerful barrier to the polls: Senate Enrolled Act (SEA) 483, for which every Democrat voted Nay and every Republican Aye.

Among other things, this 2006 law required government-issued photo ID to vote; defined what types of identification were acceptable; and offered to provide, at state expense, an identification card to those who could not afford it.

The American Civil Liberties Union (ACLU), the NAACP, and Indiana's Democratic Party immediately challenged SEA 483. They maintained that it was unjustified given that there was no proof of rampant voter fraud. They held that SEA 483 was aimed at disenfranchising as many people of color as possible. The case went all the way to the US Supreme Court. The case was *Crawford v. Marion County Election Board*. Opening arguments commenced January 9, 2008.

Before the High Court, the ACLU and NAACP went right after the core of the issue—there was no voter fraud! Indiana had not given evidence of a *single* instance. Since statehood in 1816, not one living soul had been charged with the crime of voter impersonation. There were, of course, the same old tried-and-true anecdotes, but the stories had been debunked. So, asked the ACLU and NAACP attorneys, what "state interest" could possibly justify the burdens placed on citizens' right to vote—the burden of getting a state-issued photo ID?

In its response, Indiana assured the court, among other things, that only 1 percent of Indiana's voting-age eligible population lacked the necessary identification. And, most important, it claimed that the law had not dampened voter turnout at all. In fact, the state pointed to a study showing that in 2006, the voter turnout actually increased.

The NAACP and ACLU countered that the state's numbers, study, and analysis were nonsense.

Take the 1 percent of eligible voters who lacked an ID. That was nothing to take lightly: it represented 43,000 citizens. What's more, the attorneys presented a recent survey of Indiana voters that "found that approximately 16% . . . did not have either a current license or state identification card and 13% of current registered voters did not have licenses or identification cards." In fact, a subsequent study found that in Indiana, "white citizens were 11.5 percentage points more likely than black citizens to have the accepted credentials to vote," reported the Center for American Progress.

The situation was exacerbated by the state's "Byzantine requirements imposed on persons attempting to obtain identification from the BMV [Bureau of Motor Vehicles]. . . . In a given week 60% of applicants for licenses or state identification cards are turned away because they fail to have the appropriate documents mandated by the BMV."

So, sure, the state offered "free" IDs. But documents required to obtain one were not so easy to get and often came with costs borne solely by the would-be voter. The NAACP and ACLU noted, for example, that a birth certificate was necessary to get a driver's license, but in an obvious "Catch-22 of classic proportions" in Marion County, where more than two hundred thousand of the state's black population lived, the health department required a driver's license as proof of identification to get a copy of a birth certificate. The tangle of rules, regulations, and the state voter ID law had consequences—real-life consequences.

The attorneys told, for example, the story of Therese Clemente, who "made multiple fruitless trips to her local BMV in an effort to present the proper combination of documents in order to be able to vote."

The ACLU and NAACP attorneys laid out information about the limited number of BMVs, the scarcity of public transportation to get to those scattered facilities, and the difficulty and costs of obtaining a birth certificate. They worked to explain how this innocuous-sounding law was a targeted hit, especially for those who did not have the financial resources to amass the documentation to get the necessary ID. The NAACP and ACLU noted the strong correlation between race and poverty in Indiana and they maintained that SEA 483 would strip those populations of their basic right to vote.

In the end, studies and statistics were not enough.

The stories not enough.

The data not enough.

As far as the majority of the justices were concerned, what the NAACP and the ACLU identified as a "constitutional danger sign" was no more than smoke and mirrors, while the mythical beast of voter fraud was real. On April 28, 2008, in a 6–3 decision, the High Court ruled that the state's needs were compelling and there was no concomitant evidence that SEA 483 placed any substantive burden on voters to block their access to the polls. Indiana's voter ID law was, under this reasoning, constitutional.

And then there's the Peach State.

Georgia, though still under the Voting Rights Act's preclearance mandate, crafted its voter ID law in 2005. Its version got rid of twelve types of acceptable identification to vote, including utility bills, bank statements, and private employer IDs. It put in their place a list of six types of government-issued photo IDs. As a state website tells us, they are:

- Any valid state or federal government–issued photo ID, including a free ID Card issued by your county registrar's office or the Georgia Department of Driver Services (DDS)

- Georgia Driver's License, even if expired
- Valid employee photo ID from any branch, department, agency, or entity of the U.S. Government, Georgia, or any county, municipality, board, authority, or other entity of this state
- Valid U.S. passport ID
- Valid U.S. military photo ID
- Valid tribal photo ID

Thus, only a few short years after the passage of HAVA, a preclearance state took a virtual machete to the federal law's much more expansive list of IDs and created a stump of severely curtailed acceptable forms of identification to vote.

Because that stump had a clear racial bias, black and Latino lawmakers' concerns were ignored as white Republicans steamrolled this legislation, HB 244 (for House Bill 244), through the statehouse.

People of color had raised the need for voter education on the new requirements.

They had voiced concern about the uneven distribution of driver's license bureaus throughout the state.

They had explained the difficulty for those not born in hospitals to get a birth certificate that would allow them to get a license.

All to no avail.

Indeed, despite Georgia's Section 5 status, the state was beyond cavalier in considering the racial implications of the change in voter ID requirements. According to the DOJ, Susan Lacetti Meyers, chief policy adviser to the Georgia House of Representatives, said that the legislature "did not conduct any statistical analysis of the effect of the photo ID requirement on minority voters." In fact, when asked about the need for this law, Representative Sue Burmeister from Augusta explained that it was to prevent fraud and if the voter ID law led to fewer black voters, it was because there was "less opportunity for fraud."

Even a sentiment so racist, however, couldn't damage HB 244's momentum. The state's GOP had been fed voter-fraud talking points by a well-resourced, well-coordinated group of right-wing activists, such as John Fund, whose book *Stealing Elections* was one of the bibles for demanding photo IDs to vote.

Staff attorneys in the DOJ's Civil Rights Division had actually rejected HB 244 because of its harm to black voters. Their investigation found that only one-third of Georgia's counties had a Department of Driver Services (DDS). Added to that, Atlanta had not even one. Moreover, of Georgia's fifty-six DDS locations, folks could only get to five via public transportation. For the other fifty-one, no vehicle, no go.

As the attorneys dug deeper into the data, they uncovered that 17.7 percent of black households did not have access to a vehicle as opposed to 4.4 percent of white households. Even more troubling were the statistics in the two counties that Atlanta spread across—Fulton and DeKalb. In Fulton, almost *three-fourths* of those without a vehicle were black people. In DeKalb, the figure was 63.5 percent. Similar analysis on poverty rates, access to birth certificates, and unemployment rates (given that government work IDs were acceptable) resulted in the same pattern of racial inequality that would easily impact the ability to vote.

On August 25, 2005, DOJ attorneys recommended that HB 244 be rejected "on the ground that the state has failed to meet its burden of proof to demonstrate that it does not have the effect of retrogressing minority voting strength."

But HB 244 had friends at the DOJ. For one, political appointee John Tanner, the chief of the Voting Section of the Civil Rights Division.

The day after DOJ attorneys gave HB 244 the thumbs-down, Tanner overruled them and allowed Georgia to implement what would become one of the "strictest" voter ID laws in the United States, according to Suevon Lee and Sarah Smith in a post for ProPublica, a not-for-profit news outlet that specializes in investigative journalism.

After the election of President Barack Obama, Republicans amped up their efforts to pass voter ID laws.

10

FLOODGATES OPENED WIDE

THE ELECTION OF BARACK OBAMA TO THE PRESI-
dency on November 4, 2008, increased GOP zeal for the very
effective tool of disenfranchisement that voter ID is. Fifteen million new voters came to the polls in 2008. They were overwhelmingly black, Latino, Asian, and poor. Sixty-nine percent of these
new participants in democracy voted for Obama, and, as a result,
America had its first black president.

All that hope for change, though, dissipated in the midst of a
recession—one like no other since the Great Depression of the
1930s—which had begun under President George W. Bush. It
had already destroyed twenty-two trillion dollars of wealth,
fueled and entrenched double-digit unemployment for black
people, and led to economic stimulus packages that were targeted
at banks and other financial institutions whose greed and recklessness had put the global economy in a tailspin.

There was also a cabal of obstructionist and extremist

Republicans whose sole mission was to see to it that Obama was a one-term president. As a result, in the 2010 midterm elections the GOP swept several long-term Democrats out of Congress, picking up six seats in the Senate and sixty-three in the House of Representatives, and adding six governors to the roster. As the *Washington Post* reported on November 13, 2010, "before the midterm elections, Democrats controlled 27 state legislatures outright. Republicans were in charge in 14 states, and eight states were split. (Nebraska, which has a single legislative chamber, is officially nonpartisan.) Today, Republicans control 26 state legislatures, Democrats 17, and five states have split control. In New York officials are still determining who is in charge of the state senate." It was, without question, a political bloodbath. (As for the New York senate, Republicans came away with a 32–30 majority.)

In 2011 and 2012, the floodgates opened wide for voter ID laws. According to Nancy MacLean in her award-winning book *Democracy in Chains: The Deep History of the Radical Right's Stealth Plan for America*, "180 bills to restrict who could vote and how" appeared in forty-one states. "Most of these bills," wrote MacLean, "seemed aimed at low-income voters, particularly minority voters, and at young people and the less mobile elderly." As one investigation put it, "the country hadn't seen anything like it since the end of Reconstruction, when every southern state placed severe limits on the franchise."

The group behind this well-coordinated effort was the American Legislative Exchange Council (ALEC), founded back in the 1970s by a man who once declared that he didn't want "everybody to vote." In 2009, ALEC began to draft model voter

ID legislation. With the GOP in control of more than half the nation's state governments after the 2010 midterm elections, these bills arose like dragon's teeth out of the soil of racism and disenfranchisement—out of a Republican vision of democracy that views most citizens as unworthy.

Iowa congressman Steve King lamented the passing of "a time in American history when you had to be a male property owner in order to vote."

The point was to eliminate the voters who were resistant to right-wing policies and so produce a much smoother road to re-create the civil rights order of the early 1950s and the economic environment of unregulated capitalism of the 1920s.

Two key US Supreme Court decisions greased the path. One was the *Shelby County v. Holder* decision (2013), which gutted the Voting Rights Act of 1965. Prior to this ruling, as Justice Ruth Bader Ginsburg's dissent noted, "between 1982 and 2006, DOJ objections blocked over 700 voting changes based on a determination that the changes were discriminatory." The DOJ's findings were reinforced during congressional hearings on the 2006 reauthorization of the VRA. There it became apparent that those proposed changes that the DOJ had denied were actually the preclearance states' "calculated decisions to keep minority voters from fully participating in the political process." And now that protection was gone.

The other key US Supreme Court decision was *Citizens United v. Federal Election Commission* (2010). Here the High Court ruled that the laws that limited corporate donations to political campaigns actually violated businesses' right to free speech. The flood of hundreds of millions of virtually untraceable dollars, so-called dark money, poured into the coffers of the GOP.

Now that the Republicans controlled most of the states' electoral machinery as well as Congress, they continued to saturate the air with the lie of massive voter fraud until "nearly half of Americans believe voter fraud happens at least somewhat often, and 70 percent think it happens at least occasionally," wrote Michael Wines in a 2016 *New York Times* piece.

While many Americans came to accept the lie as truth, there was no evidence that it was the scourge of democracy that Republicans had portrayed. The real threat was the damage this lie did to governance and to the sanctity of the right to vote. Todd Allbaugh, an aide to a Republican state senator in Wisconsin, recoiled when, during a discussion of several voter ID bills, he saw how, he wrote on a Facebook post, "a handful of GOP Senators were giddy about the ramifications and literally singled out the prospects of suppressing minority and college voters. Think about that for a minute. Elected officials planning and happy to deny a fellow American's constitutional right to vote in order to increase their own chances to hang onto power."

This was no one-off. In a series of April 6, 2011, emails where Republicans were concerned that their candidate for the Wisconsin Supreme Court, Judge David Prosser, just might lose, GOP operatives, as one outlet reported, began plotting:

Steve Baas, a lobbyist for the Metropolitan Milwaukee Association of Commerce and former Republican legislative staffer, floated an idea on the email thread: "Do we need to start messaging 'widespread reports of election fraud' so we are positively set up for the recount regardless of the final number? I obviously think we should." Scott Jensen—the former GOP Assembly Speaker turned lobbyist for American Federation for Children, a private school voucher advocacy group—quickly responded: "Yes. Anything fishy should be highlighted. Stories should be solicited by talk radio hosts." In another email, Jensen writes that [Judge] Prosser "needs to be on talk radio in the morning saying he is confident he won and talk radio needs to scream the Dems are trying to steal the race."

The bogeyman of voter fraud has also proven useful in North Carolina, where Republican governor Pat McCrory insisted that the only way to keep the monster at bay was the draconian ID law his state instituted. But an analysis by the North Carolina State Board of Elections of nearly 4.8 million votes in the 2016 election found only one vote that was fraudulent and could have possibly been stopped by voter ID.

The story was the same across the United States. Law professor Justin Levitt conducted an extensive study and uncovered that from 2000 to 2014, there were thirty-one voter impersonation cases out of *one billion* votes nationwide. But the lie of voter fraud remains a salient part of the American political landscape

The effectiveness of voter ID laws is based on three key features.

Number 1: From the very beginning, the dog whistle target has been "urban" areas with large populations of people of color. Kit Bond railed against electoral corruption in St. Louis. ACVR identified a rogue's gallery of cities where millions of black

Americans lived, including some where they were the majority population. Representative Burmeister singled out blacks in Augusta who were supposedly willing to sell their votes. Psychologically, the word association of "crime," "urban," and "African Americans" made the connection of "stealing" an election via fraud cognitively palpable to the broader population, which had linked crime and blackness together for ages.

Number 2: Supposedly respectable members of society leveled the charges. US senators, attorneys with law degrees from Ivy League schools, governors, and others fervently and doggedly warned the nation about voter fraud, voter fraud, voter fraud. The credibility of those accusations was amplified by newscasts that did not question the assertions of voter fraud but simply reported them.

Number 3: For the broader public who didn't question this threat, the response seemed measured, reasonable, and commonsensical.

Numbers 1, 2, and 3 combined to provide ample cover for state after state after state to systematically target and disenfranchise millions of American citizens.

In 2011, Alabama passed a photo ID law but never sought preclearance from the Department of Justice. In crafting this legislation, the state tossed out HAVA's range of valid identification such as a utility bill or social security card and homed in on only certain types of government-issued photo ID, which, disproportionately, black Americans and the poor did not have. Without preclearance, though, the law lay dormant for years. After the

2013 *Shelby County v. Holder* decision, however, Alabama's voter ID law was good to go.

Citizens were now going to have to run an obstacle course to acquire the appropriate identification to vote. For example, the state refused to accept public housing ID, although this clearly is government-issued. Because a greater percentage of black people live in public housing, this edict disproportionately affects them. Alabama is one of the poorest states in the nation, and nearly 34 percent of Latinos and 31 percent of blacks live below the poverty line, compared with 14 percent of whites.

A 2017 study by the NAACP Legal Defense and Educational Fund (NAACP LDF) found that "more than 100,000 registered voters in Alabama can't vote because they don't have the photo identification required by the state," journalist Kent Faulk reported. Most of the disenfranchised were poor, making less than ten thousand dollars a year, and were black or Latino.

As if reading from the ALEC playbook, North Carolina instituted what Ian Millhiser with the Center for American Progress called the nation's "worst voter suppression law." Driving that decision was the grim reality for the Republicans that in the twenty-first century, black voter registration had increased by 51.1 percent in the state and black people also had a higher voter turnout "rate than white registered voters in both the 2008 and 2012 presidential elections," reported Brynna Quillin in a *Kennedy School Review* post.

Republican legislators, therefore, gathered the data on the types of identification black people had and didn't have, then tailored the list of vote-worthy IDs to favor whites. Their actions were so brazen that the federal court ruled that the law was targeted at black Americans, said Judge Dianna Gribbon Motz, "with almost surgical precision." The court also blasted North Carolina's voter identification legislation as designed to "impose cures for problems that did not exist." Indeed, Judge Motz wrote that all of North Carolina's talk about the dangers of voter fraud "cannot and do not conceal the state's true motivation."

Just as North Carolina was concerned about how to stanch the growing voter turnout rate of black Americans, Texas lawmakers also set out to neutralize the sizable demographic shift in their state. With more than 80 percent of Texas urbanized, Dallas now a Democratic stronghold, and Houston and San Antonio overwhelmingly populated by people of color, it was clear that the burgeoning Latino and black population had the ability to turn a red state not just purple, but blue.

Texas's answer was SB 14 (for Senate Bill 14). The law skewed acceptable government-issued photo IDs to those "which white people are more likely to carry," such as gun licenses. It made driver's licenses the virtual holy grail of IDs because nearly one-third of the state's counties, including some of those that are heavily populated by people of color, do not have DMVs. Republican legislators recognized that it would require some citizens to travel up to 250 miles round-trip to obtain a license, but the lawmakers decided to remove language from SB 14 that would have reimbursed those who had to make that poll tax–like trip. In fact, one of the state's lawyers "brushed aside geographical obstacles as the 'reality to life of choosing to live in that part of Texas.'"

The NAACP and its Legal Defense and Educational Fund, meanwhile, were left to deal with the six hundred thousand black, Latino, and poor voters who were currently registered but did not have the required ID. And, even more frightening for the future of democracy in Texas, an additional one million, who had not yet registered, also lacked any of the identification on the state's "exceptionally narrow" list. State officials, such as Governor Greg Abbott, were determined to keep it that way and refused to provide any substantive funding or resources to help the situation.

The goal of all the GOP voter ID laws is to reduce significantly the demographic and political impact of a growing share of the American electorate, to diminish people's ability to choose government representatives and the types of policies they support. Unfortunately, it's working. In 2017 *Newsweek* reported that a study showed that "the turnout gaps between white and ethnic minority voters are far higher in states where people must show ID during or after voting." There is a 4.9 percent gap between Latino and white voters in states that do not require an ID, but this "leaps to a 13.2 percent" difference in states like Texas, North Carolina, Georgia, and Wisconsin. For African Americans, the gap "rises from 2.9 percent to 5.1 percent; among Asians, the gap increases from 6.5 percent to 11.5 percent." In Wisconsin, 8.3 percent of white voters who were surveyed said they were "deterred" from voting in the 2016 election because of voter ID laws; that number more than tripled for African Americans (27.5 percent).

A Government Accountability Office report, wrote journalist Sarah Childress in 2014, "suggests that voter ID laws are having an impact at the polls. Turnout dropped among both young people and African-Americans in Kansas and Tennessee after new voter ID requirements took effect in 2012."

Another study posits, however, that it's not the advent of voter ID laws but the confusion over what the correct identification is that actually drives down voter turnout. This also explains why states such as Texas, Georgia, and Indiana have mightily resisted expending virtually any resources on voter education about the new standards. Wisconsin, in fact, used a federal court's ruling that upended the state's ID law to sow even greater confusion about what the revised guidelines, post-court decision, actually were. The state's flat-out refusal to train the staff at the Department of Motor Vehicles on the new court-ordered requirements left Wisconsinites "at the mercy" of DMV employees who had no idea about the necessary documents and IDs required to vote.

The state's willful defiance also led to a harsh rebuke from the judge who had already called Wisconsin's efforts at credentialing voters a "wretched failure" because of the disparate impact on black and Latino Americans.

The results of the confusion and defiance of a federal court order were predictable: a precipitous decline in voter turnout in 2016, especially in the overwhelmingly black, Democratic stronghold of Milwaukee.

The lie of voter fraud breaks a Korean War veteran down into making a simple, horrifying statement: "I wasn't a citizen no more."

It forces a retired engineer into facing a bitter truth: "I am not wanted in this state."

It eviscerates the key sense of self-worth in a disabled man who has to pen the painful words "My constitutional rights have been stripped from me."

It brands thousands of black Americans who have resiliently weathered election day lines and hours of bureaucratic run-arounds as nothing but criminals and frauds.

★ PART THREE ★

VOTER ROLL PURGE

Georgia's then-secretary of state Brian Kemp led the charge against alleged voter fraud in 2016.

11

AND KEMP SAW DEAD PEOPLE

VIRGINIA: 41,637 PURGED SHORTLY BEFORE ELEC-tion Day 2014.

Indiana: 481,235 purged between Election Day 2016 and April 2017.

Georgia: 591,548 purged over a weekend in late July 2017.

Ohio: two million purged between 2011 and 2016.

Millions of Americans—veterans, congressional representatives, judges, county officials, and most decidedly people of color—were erased from the voting rolls.

Casualties in the war on democracy—people denied their right to vote by a GOP deftly wielding a law that had actually been designed to *broaden access to the polls.*

The law is the National Voter Registration Act (NVRA), created in the aftermath of the dismal turnout for the 1988 presidential contest between Democrat Michael Dukakis and Republican George H. W. Bush. It was one of the lowest voter-turnout rates since 1924. Approximately 91.3 million, barely half of eligible Americans, voted.

Why?

"When there's no organizing structures to help people get registered," observed Columbia University professor Richard Cloward, "the voter registration barriers just sort of gradually erode the electorate." In other words, when registering to vote is a hassle, many people—people with unforgiving bosses, people working two or three jobs, people with children or spouses or parents to care for—many of these people simply throw in the towel.

In some counties in Mississippi, for example, the only place to register to vote was in the clerk's office during traditional business hours of nine to five. For people who work during that time, it can be impossible to get to the office and back during a lunch break. In Indianapolis, Indiana, voter registration drives were hampered by a "rule" that doled out a maximum of twenty-five forms to each volunteer.

Limited access to registration had a visible and disparate impact on the voting public. According to a report by Demos, a progressive think tank, while top income brackets achieved about 80 percent voter registration rates, "from 1972 to 1992, voter registration among the lowest income quintile saw a nearly 18 percentage point drop—from 61.2 percent in 1972 to 43.5 percent in 1992."

To amp up voter participation, in 1993 Congress passed the NVRA, also known as the Motor Voter law. The National Voter Registration Act's opening preamble is clear. The right to vote "is a fundamental right" of US citizens. And, it is "the duty of the

Federal, State, and local government to promote the exercise of that right." This obligation requires paying particular attention to "discriminatory and unfair registration laws and procedures" that "can have a direct and damaging effect on voter participation" and "disproportionately harm voter participation by various groups, including racial minorities."

To this end, the NVRA expanded the places where people could register to vote and standardized the process of registration. Now citizens could register at the Department of Motor Vehicles as well as at public assistance and disability offices. People could also register through the mail with a brand-new standardized federal form. In just a few years the number of registered voters increased nationwide by more than 3.3 million.

But there was a devil in the NVRA's details, and a diabolical reason that there was such a lag time between the initial concern in 1988 about the dismal voter turnout and the passage of the law in 1993.

During the negotiations, Republicans at first stalled, then demanded, in exchange for their support, that the law require routine maintenance—scrubbing even—of the voter rolls. This would ensure that people who had moved out of a district or a state and those who had died were no longer listed as eligible voters. It all sounded so reasonable and so mundane.

Except it wasn't.

What the law requires and how it has been implemented are two different things.

The NVRA mandates that election officials update the voter rolls regularly. But there are strict guidelines about who is removed, how that is accomplished, and why. The NVRA out-lines that officials can remove someone from the roll of eligible voters if . . .

- he or she requests it;
- he or she has had a name change and didn't notify authorities within ninety days;
- he or she dies;
- he or she is convicted of a felony that under state law renders them ineligible to vote;
- he or she "has moved outside the county of registration or has registered to vote in another jurisdiction";

and

- he or she fails to respond to a follow-up inquiry, usually a mailing, from election officials concerning a change in status. Then, and only then, is the process of purging supposed to begin.

In other words, the NVRA mandates a *two-step* process trig-gered (1) by a change in status of the voter (name change, felony conviction, move) and (2) by an inquiry from a state election official about his or her continued eligibility to vote in that jurisdiction.

Unfortunately, far too many secretaries of state have bypassed this carefully laid-out two-step process. Instead they used *one* spe-cific criterion to wipe out otherwise eligible voters: Non-voting.

Non-voting is not among the above bullet points. What's more, to purge someone from the voter rolls solely for not voting is expressly forbidden in the NVRA.

The point of this illegal tactic is to cull the electorate of millions of citizens, most of whom are young, poor, and/or people of color, who statistically do not vote for Republicans and whose voting activities are often sporadic.

Ohio has been in the forefront of this lethal maneuver. In fact, no state has been more aggressive or more consistent in attacking the heart of the NVRA. From 2011 to 2016, its secretary of state Jon Husted wiped two million people from the state's list of registered voters. Of that number, 1.2 million citizens were eliminated solely because they voted infrequently. Yet the NVRA is crystal clear: people cannot be struck from the registration rolls simply because they did not vote in a few federal elections.

Larry Harmon of Kent, Ohio, a white man who is a software engineer and Navy veteran, was one of the millions of Americans punished for sitting out elections. In 2008, Harmon eagerly voted for Barack Obama. In 2012, he was somewhat disenchanted with President Obama and partially swayed by Republican challenger Mitt Romney's platform. Unable to choose, Harmon sat out the election. When the 2014 midterm elections came around, Harmon was not impressed with any of the candidates for Congress. Again he stayed home. Then came 2015.

There was a local initiative concerning legalized marijuana on the ballot, and Harmon, age fifty-nine, wanted his voice to be heard on the issue, so he went to vote only to be told that he couldn't because he wasn't registered to vote.

At first, Harmon "felt embarrassed and stupid," then angry. How could he simply be erased like that? As he dug deeper, as he learned that the constitutionally protected act of *not voting* had just cost him his right to vote, Harmon became infuriated.

The man had not been living off the grid.

He had been paying his taxes and registering his car.

He still lived in the same house, on the same block, in the same jurisdiction.

He hadn't changed his name. He was Larry Harmon in 2008. He remained Larry Harmon in 2015.

And he clearly had not died.

> "I'm a veteran, my father's a veteran, my grandfather's a veteran, now they aren't giving me my right to vote, the most fundamental right I have? I just can't believe it."
>
> —Larry Harmon, after learning that he had been purged from voter rolls

It turns out that in 1994, Ohio had "updated its elections law to add what is known as a "'supplemental process'" to the NVRA, explained Leigh Chapman, senior policy advisor at Let America Vote. "Simply put, voters may be purged from the rolls after six years just because they didn't vote—even if they are otherwise eligible." Ohio, in other words, had flipped federal law on its head.

Ohio secretary of state Jon Husted argued that his office had fulfilled its obligations. It had mailed postcards to Harmon and millions like him alerting them that if they did not respond within thirty days, the process of removal would begin. "If this is really [an] important thing to you in your life, voting," Husted chided, "you probably would have done so within a six-year period."

As for those mailings Husted was apparently so proud of . . .

Mailing postcards crammed with fine print is fraught with discriminatory impact. The Census Bureau, for example, uncovered that when it sends out mail, "white voters are 21 percent more likely than blacks or Hispanics to respond to their official requests; homeowners are 32 percent more likely to respond than renters; and the young are 74 percent less likely than the old to respond," wrote investigative journalist Greg Palast in a 2016 article for *Rolling Stone*, "The GOP's Stealth War Against Voters." Clearly, postcards with fine print don't only trip up people of color, renters, and young people. After all, Larry Harmon was white and a homeowner. But, the differential response rates for Husted's mailings translate into disproportionate purges in key neighborhoods of Cleveland, Columbus, and Cincinnati—areas that are overwhelmingly populated by people of color and composed of renters and young adults.

Take Cleveland. In 2016, whites made up 34.5 percent of its residents, while 49.1 percent were black and 11 percent Latino. Moreover, nearly 60 percent of homes in the city are occupied by renters. It is also a town where 69 percent of the voters went for Obama in 2012. By 2016, however, the percentage of voters for the Democratic candidate had dropped to 66 percent, while the Republican share stayed virtually the same. That little bit of magic might be explained by the fact that, as Reuters reported, "voters in neighborhoods that backed Obama by more than 60 percent in 2012" had more than twice as many registered voters purged "for inactivity" than "neighborhoods where Obama got less than 40 percent of the vote." Indeed, more than one-fourth of the two hundred thousand Ohioans Husted purged from the voter rolls in 2015 were in Cuyahoga County alone, where Cleveland is located.

Husted's insistence that if a person cared about voting "you probably would have done so within a six-year period" flies in the face of the fact that not voting regularly is not solely an individual choice or a question of people being slackers.

For years, Ohio has taken an active role in dissuading citizens from voting or even having those votes count. Secretary of State Husted and his Republican predecessor Kenneth Blackwell have, for example, limited the number of polling stations for early voting in urban areas with larger populations of people of color, thus creating four- to five-hour wait times. These election officials have also tossed tens of thousands of absentee ballots, supposedly for reasons such as having spelling errors. In a deposition, Husted's top aide admitted that these so-called enforcement activities were actually targeted at the cities, while "white rural areas went nearly untouched."

Ohio is not alone. Georgia and politican Brian Kemp have also mastered the art of the purge. Georgia has been so good at it that even as its population climbed, its number of registered voters since 2012 has actually dropped.

Yet again, the battle cry was Voter Fraud!

During his time as secretary of state, Kemp led a crusade against voter fraud, including "investigat[ing] voter-registration drives by Asian American and predominately black groups," wrote Michael Wines in a July 2016 *New York Times* article. Kemp actually launched a criminal inquiry into the registration of 85,000 new voters, "many of them minorities," continued Wines, but "found problems with only 25 of the registrants." And here's the kicker. After all the time, money, and publicity, "no charges were filed."

Yet the intimidation was real—too real and too familiar for black folks.

Georgia's perfidy has not gone unnoticed and has resulted in an onslaught of lawsuits from the NAACP, the ACLU, and the League of Women Voters. Kemp's response, however, has been Orwellian. Confronted with 732,800 voters who, between October 2012 and November 2014, had their "registration status canceled 'due to failure to vote'" and then another 591,548 who were wiped off the rolls just two years later, Candice Broce, a spokeswoman for Kemp's office, took umbrage at the charge of purging the rolls and explained that the "secretary of state's office does not 'purge' any voters." That's just not a word that his office was willing to use. Instead, his staff explained, in language that the public was meant to find reassuring, the elimination of more than one million citizens from the rolls was nothing more than "voter list maintenance . . . to safeguard . . . the integrity of the ballot box . . . and prevent fraud and ensure that all votes are cast by eligible Georgia voters."

And Kemp saw dead people.

The charge that waves of folks impersonate the dead to cast ballots in Georgia has been disproved repeatedly. Political scientists M. V. Hood III from the University of Georgia and William Gillespie from Kennesaw State University concluded that, after "examining approximately 2.1 million votes cast during the 2006 general election in Georgia, we find no evidence that election fraud was committed under the auspices of deceased registrants."

A decade after that election, the *Washington Post* reported that despite all the baying at the moon, there were no cases prosecuted in Georgia for voter impersonation fraud.

Kemp, however, did not hesitate to raise the bogeyman of voter fraud to mask the state's voter suppression efforts. The subterfuge continued as the secretary of state explained the rationale for wiping more than one million citizens from the rolls. Kemp argued that he was merely following state law and that the criterion for removal was simply that the voter had had no contact with election officials over a span of seven years, not, as his critics charged, because of non-voting. The hocus-pocus in that statement is obvious. If a citizen doesn't move and doesn't change his or her name, there is absolutely no reason to contact the secretary of state's office. None. It is not about changes of address or even name changes; it's realizing that people of color, the poor, and the young are less likely to vote than affluent whites are.

And there are the monstrous programs Exact Match and Crosscheck.

Karen Handel, Georgia's secretary of state in 2007, enacted Exact Match, which demanded that names in the voter registration database and the state's Department of Motor Vehicle records match precisely.

12

EXACT MATCH AND CROSSCHECK

BACK IN MARCH 2007, WHEN KAREN HANDEL, Republican, was Georgia's secretary of state, the Peach State mandated Exact Match. Using the bogeyman of voter fraud and the cover of the NVRA's requirement for voter roll maintenance, Georgia insisted that the names in its voter registration database match those in the Department of Motor Vehicles database in every way. But there were at least two problems with the Exact Match plan.

First, at the time, Georgia was under the preclearance provision of the VRA and hadn't bothered to ask the Department of Justice for approval. Yet because the counsel to the head of the Civil Rights Division, Hans von Spakovsky (appointed by Republican president George W. Bush) had, over the strenuous objections of the career attorneys at the DOJ, already approved Georgia's voter ID law, the state assumed that it had little to fear when it came to employing Exact Match.

Second, the databases of the DMV and secretary of state's offices were fraught with errors—a missing "e" in the name Carole, a hyphen where one was not supposed to be, an errant "y" instead of an "i" in Nicki, or any of the other numerous typographical errors that can happen when two large bureaucracies are processing millions of applications.

All this had a horrific effect on voter registration, especially for people of color. "Of nearly 35,000 registration forms that were canceled or placed in 'pending status' for the data mismatches from July 2013 to July 2016, nearly 64 percent were submitted by blacks," wrote journalist Tony Pugh. Added to that, "Asian-Americans and Latinos were more than six times as likely as white voters to have their applications halted."

The devastation of Georgia's Exact Match was amplified in nearly thirty states by the Interstate Voter Registration Crosscheck program, commonly called simply Crosscheck.

Interstate Crosscheck began in 2005 as a small, regional endeavor. In many ways, the premise was the same as Exact Match: the alignment of databases would be able to flag fraudulent voters and purge them from the rolls. For a few years, the program limped along, virtually unnoticed.

Enter Kris Kobach. He embarked on a mission to make Crosscheck more robust, more pronounced, and, frankly, more electorally lethal.

Kris Kobach, a Harvard, University of Oxford, and Yale Law School grad, exuded certainty that America was under attack from brown immigrants and black voters. There was, as a result, a zealotry to all of Kobach's work. He "has been a key architect behind many of the nation's anti-voter and anti-immigration policies," observed Tomas Lopez and Jennifer L. Clark in a Brennan Center for Justice post. Back in 2001 when Kobach was at the DOJ, he developed a database screening program to identify Muslims as terrorist threats. Though thousands were deported, no terrorists were ever found. But Kobach called the program a "great success." After he left the DOJ, he eventually moved on to Arizona to help bolster the infamous "Driving While Brown" anti-immigrant law that made Maricopa County's sheriff Joe Arpaio so notorious.

Riding on the wave of his reputation in staunch conservative circles, in 2010 Kobach ran to be Kansas's secretary of state. As Ari Berman reported, Kobach told the *Kansas City Star* that "My hope is that Kansas will be to stopping election fraud what Arizona is to stopping illegal immigration."

Once he was elected secretary of state, Kobach's first battle cry was a menacing thrust at the voter fraud that had purportedly engulfed Kansas. As "Exhibit A," he pointed to a case where a man named Albert Brewer, who had been dead for years, showed up and voted in the previous primary election. Kobach held up this instance as one of thousands lurking in the voter rolls, skewing elections and canceling out legitimate votes from hardworking, honest Americans. It was vintage Kobach, vintage GOP. It was also not true.

Yes, there was an Albert Brewer who had died. And there was one who voted. But they were not one and the same person.

The Albert Brewer who voted—Albert Brewer Jr.—was the son of the man who had died. Kobach hadn't even bothered to check before he started slinging accusations.

That kind of deliberate sloppiness would, however, be his trademark. It's the way he garnered the support necessary to wipe thousands off the rolls in Kansas and millions throughout the United States. In the 2016 election, Kobach's office rejected more ballots than even Florida did—a state with a population seven times larger than that of Kansas. That sledgehammer approach makes clear that Kobach's goal was not to get it right. The goal was to tilt the electorate to the right. Said Missouri's former secretary of state Jason Kander in 2017: "Kobach uses every trick that he can to make it as hard as possible for eligible voters to cast a ballot—whether it's unconstitutional legislation, targeting immigrants or forcing more eligible voters to use provisional ballots."

Kobach helped draft a 2011 Kansas law based on the lies of voter fraud and immigrant takeover of the ballot box. This law is the absolutely misnamed Secure and Fair Elections (SAFE) Act. As scholar Chelsie Bright explained, under SAFE, the state required a voter to "1) present photo IDs prior to casting a ballot, 2) present a full driver's license number and have their signatures verified in order to absentee vote and 3) provide proof of citizenship to register to vote."

Number 3, which could be satisfied with a birth certificate or a US passport, was supposed to address the fear of noncitizens voting in elections. Although, as one politician noted, immigrants don't "com[e] here to vote. . . . They come here to work," Kobach insisted that they were stealing elections or, equally frightening, were more than capable of doing so. "We had margins of less than 10 for water commissioner, school board and mayors," Kobach claimed. And, with eighteen thousand noncitizens supposedly poised to usurp the rights of Americans, immigrants could take over key positions in government. Kobach led a hunt for culprits. He turned Kansas upside down, wrangling prosecutorial power from the legislature, but found only a Peruvian immigrant who was actually in the process of naturalizing and erroneously thought he could cast a ballot.

One lone immigrant cannot and simply does not convey a widespread problem. So, the secretary of state billed it as "the tip of the iceberg."

Kobach, therefore, suspended the right to vote of 35,314 Kansans because they could not produce "proof of U.S. citizenship." More than 12,000 of those he simply purged outright because the disparate access to citizenship documents played right into Kobach's belief about who is American and who is not, and thus, who has the right to vote. He "associated minority voters with 'ethnic cleansing,'" pointed out Sherrilyn Ifill, president of the NAACP's LDF. In 2014, Kobach described "a conspiracy to replace American voters with illegal aliens."

The US Commission on Civil Rights rightfully concluded that the SAFE Act "may disparately impact voters on the basis of age, sex, disability, race, income level and affiliation." And, the commission continued, what it costs, especially for the poor, to obtain a passport or a birth certificate is a "barrier" that amounts to "an unconstitutional poll tax."

Kobach sneered that the commission's report "is not worth the paper that it was written on." Yet a study by the Brennan

Center for Justice found that "7 percent of Americans, mostly minorities, do not have these [citizenship] documents readily available." Moreover, as scholar Chelsie Bright explained, "it is unclear that proof of citizenship requirements actually add any real value to the integrity of the election process. Federal law already requires that individuals registering to vote affirm in writing that they are a US citizen. Lying carries serious criminal penalties. Further, research consistently finds that voting by non-citizens is extremely rare."

The ACLU sued. Kobach's purge was not driven by any exigent need or crisis. There was no threat to the integrity of the ballot box. In October 2016, the Tenth Circuit of the US Court of Appeals agreed. It found Kobach's hue and cry about noncitizens voting to be "pure speculation."

Yet Kobach was undeterred. He set up a two-tiered federal/state registration form and continued to harangue registrants for proof of US citizenship to vote in the state's elections.

One of those registrants was white ninety-one-year-old World War II veteran Marvin Brown, who had been around long enough to remember the poll tax. When Kobach deigned to question whether "Brown was truly a citizen," the veteran found an ally in the ACLU and went to court. There, US District judge Julie Robinson chided that Kobach once again had "scant evidence of noncitizen voter fraud." Unfazed by what would be yet another one of his losses to the American Civil Liberties Union, Kobach continued to work toward disenfranchising as many "threats" to American democracy as he could find. In fact, he had already "block[ed] 18,000 motor voter applicants from registering to vote in Kansas."

His most devastating weapon to date, however, has been Crosscheck, which he has nurtured and promoted as an important device to eliminate voter fraud from the American political landscape. The program is supposed to root out those who are registered to vote in two different states as part of "a national move to bring more integrity to the voter rolls" and provide a solution to "registration systems [that] cannot keep up with a society of voters who move from state to state." It works through an alliance of twenty-seven states, which sends voter information to Arkansas to upload. Kobach's Kansas then pulls and runs the data for every member of the consortium, searching for comparisons "of registered voters to weed out duplicates."

Crosscheck, which by 2012 had more than forty-five million voter records, matches first, middle, and last names, date of birth, last four digits of the social security number, and suffix, if applicable, to identify those who may be going from state to state to vote, tainting election after election.

At least that's the narrative Kobach told when he stumbled upon Lincoln L. Wilson, a sixty-six-year-old Republican who owned homes in both Kansas and Colorado. Wilson felt he was well within his rights to vote in local elections in both states. "I'd vote for president in one state, and local issues in both places," Wilson explained, especially when he saw his property tax bill skyrocket and resolved that there would be no taxation without representation. What looked logical to Wilson, however, and, frankly, not that much of a big deal to the local prosecutor, was a red flag to Kobach, who pursued charges against the elderly man with a vengeance. Kobach simply needed to make an example of him.

Eighteen months and nearly $50,000 in legal fees, a $6,000 fine, $158 in court costs, and a guilty plea to three misdemeanors later, Kobach had his victory. Wilson simmered, saying, "Kris Kobach came after me for an honest mistake. . . . Damn right, I'm upset. . . . I'm a convicted man now."

Wilson, however, was in many ways a fluke. Crosscheck is such a fundamentally flawed database that its "success" rate is actually an epic fail for democracy. Since the database's launch, 7.2 million voters have been flagged as suspect. Based on the individual lists the states received back from Kobach, massive purges have wiped more than one million American citizens from the electoral map.

In Virginia, for example, 342,556 names were immediately identified as suspect because they appeared to be registered in another state. Those who were already on an "inactive voters" list were summarily removed, "meaning," wrote investigative journalist Greg Palast, that "a stunning 41,637 names were 'canceled' from voter rolls, most of them just before Election Day" in November 2014.

Texas set out to purge about 80,000 voters, even though the Crosscheck match was "weak." Only a court order, prompted by a lawsuit from a man the system had marked as "dead," stopped the process.

In Ohio, Crosscheck "flagged close to half a million voters," reported Greg Palast.

In the 2016 election, it was even worse, especially given the slim popular vote margins that ultimately determined who won the Electoral College.

Arizona purged almost 271,000 voters.

Michigan removed nearly 450,000 voters, and North Carolina managed to eliminate close to 600,000 from the system.

The staggering numbers fueled the narrative of rampant voter fraud, of voter rolls so unkempt that the dead had ample opportunity to rise from the grave and tilt an election. That, of course, meant Kobach's pet program had successfully spun its web of lies, at least in the view from thirty thousand feet. But up close, neither the lists nor the database could withstand scrutiny. The problem is twofold.

First, despite the hype and the marketing, the program does not actually match on every parameter. Not all states require the same information that Crosscheck uses to purge the rolls. Social security numbers, for example, are rarely used. Ohio doesn't bother with a person's middle name. Suffixes rarely make it in, either. As a result, Crosscheck believes that James Willie Brown is the same voter as James Arthur Brown, as James Clifford Brown, as James Lynn Brown. The possibility for error is exponential. In Georgia alone, there are nearly four hundred James Browns. And in North Carolina, the supposedly more than thirty-five thousand illegal voters simply evaporated when the state hired an ex-FBI agent to ferret them out and bring them to justice. He found "exactly zero double voters from the Crosscheck list."

What's more, researchers at Stanford, Harvard, Yale, and the University of Pennsylvania discovered that Crosscheck has an error rate of more than 99 percent. The lack of consistency, rigor, and accuracy led a "shocked" Mark Swedlund, a database expert whose clients include several Fortune 500 companies, to dismiss Crosscheck's "childish methodology" after reviewing the data from Georgia and Virginia. "God forbid," he noted, if "your name is Garcia, of which there are 858,000 in the U.S. and your first name is Joseph or Jose. You're probably suspected of voting in 27 states."

Crosscheck's overreliance on a handful of selective data points feeds into the second major problem: it is a program "infected with racial and ethnic bias," as Sue Sturgis put it in a 2017 piece for *Facing South*. People of color in America tend to have common or shared last names. If your last name is Washington, for example, there is an 89 percent chance that you're black; Hernandez, a 94 percent chance that you're Latino; Kim, a 95 percent chance that you're Asian. As a result, when Crosscheck zeros in on name matches, white people are underrepresented by 8 percent on the purge lists while black people are overrepresented by 45 percent, Asian Americans by 31 percent, and Hispanics by 24 percent. With Crosscheck focusing on similar last names, it has blasted a hole through voting rights. "Roughly 14 percent of all black voters were purged from databases under the guise of preventing 'double-voting' and 'fraud,'" reported *The Root* in 2017.

The depth of disenfranchisement, of wringing the right to vote out of American citizens, led award-winning columnist Charles P. Pierce to conclude that "Kobach is Jim Crow walking." Journalist Greg Palast, after surveying the racial casualties in Ohio, knew that it wasn't just Kansas's secretary of state but an entire GOP apparatus: "It's a brand-new Jim Crow. Today, on Election Day, they're not going to use white sheets to keep away black voters. Today they're using spreadsheets."

Politician and staunch opponent of voting rights Kris Kobach meets with president-elect Donald Trump.

13

A SHAM AND A SCAM

GIVEN HIS TRACK RECORD, KRIS KOBACH SET OFF alarm bells when he stepped out of a meeting with president-elect Donald Trump in November 2016 carrying some papers that were partially visible. These papers contained talking points about how to restrict access to the polls under the new regime. Papers, by the way, that he consistently lied about and refused to produce until a court order and a thousand-dollar fine forced him to reveal that he proposed altering the NVRA to require proof of citizenship. The fears were heightened further by Trump's fantastical claim that he would have won the popular vote if it hadn't been for three million to five million illegal voters.

Concern mounted as the president, who was determined to prove his lie was the truth, signed an executive order in May 2017 creating the Presidential Advisory Commission on Election Integrity. Trump appointed as its chair Vice President Mike Pence, a man who as governor of Indiana allowed the state police to raid and destabilize an organization registering black people to vote. The commission's vice chair was Kris Kobach.

A *New York Times* editorial summed it up: the "Commission on Election Integrity . . . is a sham and a scam. It was born out of a marriage of convenience between conservative anti-voter fraud crusaders, who refuse to accept actual data, and a president who refuses to accept that he lost the popular vote fair and square."

The lie of voter fraud now had the presidential stamp of approval. It also had additional federal funding, a presidential commission, and several key members who were part of a rogue's gallery of voter suppressors.

In addition to Kobach, Kenneth Blackwell, and Hans von Spakovsky, there was J. Christian Adams. Similar to Kobach, Adams was also in Bush's Department of Justice. There he flipped the Voting Rights Act on its head and went after black Americans for supposedly violating whites' right to vote. He also made it clear that he deplored the NVRA because, in his view, "voter registration takes forethought and initiative, something lacking in large segments of the Democrat base." Under the cover of his organizations, the American Civil Rights Union (ACRU) and the Public Interest Legal Foundation (PILF), Adams bullied and targeted people of color and poor districts, and threatened lawsuit after lawsuit unless they purged their voter rolls, forcing many to capitulate because they simply didn't have the resources to fight him in court. He argued that the "Obama Administration was attempting to 'import populations with cultural and legal traditions foreign to American traditions,' and that 'noncitizen voting helps the left win elections'—statements," as the LDF's president Sherrilyn Ifill notes, "with no factual basis whatsoever."

To a commission fully packed with voter suppression crusaders, Trump, over the objections of von Spakovsky, then added a few Democrats for "window dressing." But it soon became clear that their role was to be even less than that. They were invisible.

The Democrats were blindsided by the commission's request for data from all fifty secretaries of state. In addition to voters' names, dates of birth, and the last four digits of their social security numbers, the Pence Commission—as the commission is often called—wanted party affiliation and voting patterns for every voter on the rolls, as well as information on any felony convictions.

This would have been Crosscheck on anabolic steroids, doing massive damage to the body politic by heightening and spreading the flaws in Kobach's pet database across the nation. The juiced-up pounding on Asian Americans, black Americans, and those with Hispanic surnames would have demolished their voting rights and, as much as possible, made the electorate white again. This would have been virtually assured, given the ideological, anti-black, anti-minority, anti-immigrant bent of the power center on the Pence Commission. That nationwide data in their hands spelled disenfranchisement from sea to shining sea.

The backlash to the request for more voter information was intense. There were major concerns about privacy, about the security of the database, about the intentions of the commission for amassing this data. The immediate response was that 180 people in Denver canceled their voter registration, as opposed to only 8 the previous week. There were similar cancelations in Arizona, Florida, and North Carolina.

"You are all about voter suppression to rig elections. You are evil."
—from a June 29, 2017 email
to Pence Commission staff

"This commission is a sham and Kris Kobach has been put on it expressly to disenfranchise minority voters. I am ashamed that my taxpayer dollars are being used for such purposes."
—from a June 29, 2017 email
to Pence Commission staff

"You have no right to my voting record or anyone else's; and to use it to eventually suppress voting is unconscionable in American Democracy. We saw what you did in Kansas and we are now watching you more fervently."
—from a June 29, 2017 email
to Kris Kobach

Even Republicans were alarmed. Forty-four states, including Kobach's Kansas, balked at the Pence Commission's data request. The concerns about the Pence Commission's integrity continued to mount during its first meeting in New Hampshire. Even the site was problematic. Jeffrey Toobin in the *New Yorker* observed that the "choice of this location is characteristic of the incompetence and malevolence that is at the heart of the vote-suppression agenda."

Trump had lied about thousands of Massachusetts residents coming over in buses and voting in New Hampshire, costing him and the Republican senate candidate the state in the last election. Kobach buttressed the lie and then spun a fairy tale in *Breitbart* as if voter fraud were real. It was harrowing, he wrote.

A "pivotal, close election was likely changed through voter fraud on November 8, 2016." He claimed he had "proof" that, as a *New York Times* Op-Ed said, "5,313 people who voted in New Hampshire in 2016 do not actually reside in the state." Yet, just like the 18,000 phantom noncitizens on the rolls in Kansas, just like the "massive" and "pervasive" evidence of widespread voter fraud that has yet to appear, just like the dead-then-not-so-dead Albert Brewer, who rose from the grave and voted in the primary election, Kobach's charges were once again, as the *New York Times* noted, "baseless allegations." Those 5,300-plus voters were overwhelmingly college students, whose nine-month tenure at the state's higher education institutions made them in 2016 legally eligible to vote in New Hampshire.

In addition to being built on lie after lie, the Pence Commission's shaky beginning also included getting hit with eight separate lawsuits for violating a range of federal laws about the setup and operation of government commissions. "That kind of recklessness," *Slate* columnist Mark Joseph Stern concluded, "can only heighten the widespread suspicion that the commission is interested in something other than 'election integrity.'"

The suspicion was exacerbated by the selection of witnesses called to testify during its first meeting. For a commission that, according to the vice president, "had no preconceived notions," its initial fact-finding venture featured a cavalcade of "prominent" white conservative men pounding on the "overblown charges of voter fraud."

The most controversial and telling witness, however, was a gun researcher, John Lott Jr., who advocated running voters through the same background-check system—mental health, dishonorable military discharges, substance abuse issues, and criminal history—as someone purchasing a gun. Lott's suggestion had a powerful agenda behind it. As Pema Levy and Ari Berman pointed out in *Mother Jones*, such a system would easily "deter people from voting who are distrustful of law enforcement and want to stay away from a criminal background check." Another journalist noted, in fact, that Kobach, von Spakovsky, and Lott "are playing a very serious game, burrowing into the fine print and corners of the voting process to find and exploit ways to rig the rules." Exploiting a toxic relationship with law enforcement is one way, as when Mississippi and then Florida posted sheriffs at polling places to reduce the turnout rate. Indeed, a Gallup study found that "there's a more-than-20-point gap between the portion of blacks and whites who mostly trust the police."

General distrust is one thing, but the reality of mass incarceration is another.

Its impact on voting rights is profound.

Florida governor Rick Scott exacerbated voter disenfranchisement of people convicted of felonies.

14

"A NATIONAL CHAMPION"

IN 2016, ONE IN THIRTEEN BLACK AMERICANS HAD lost their right to vote because of a felony conviction, compared with one in fifty-six non-black voters. The major villain in this set piece is the War on Drugs, which was a targeted hit on black people.

Black people in America do drugs no more than any other racial or ethnic group, yet they are imprisoned for drug charges at almost six times the rate of white people. Hyper-policing in black communities has meant that while "African Americans represent 12.5% of illicit drug users," they are "29% of those arrested for drug offenses and 33% of those incarcerated in state facilities for drug offenses," said a 2015 NAACP fact sheet.

In America, mass incarceration equals mass felony disen-franchisement. With the launch of the War on Drugs, millions of black people were swept into the criminal justice system, many

never to exercise their voting rights again. Indeed, the felony disenfranchisement rate in the United States has grown by 500 percent since 1980.

Each state has its own rules. In Vermont and Maine, there is
no felony disenfranchisement, even when the person is incarcerated. But that has little impact on the vote totals for black people,
who are only 1.3 and 1.5 percent, respectively, of those state's
populations.

The other forty-eight states have some form of disenfranchisement. Generally, the incarcerated cannot vote, but once
they have served their time, which sometimes includes parole or
probation, there is a process—often mind-boggling for the average person—that allows for the restoration of voting rights. In
2016, the Sentencing Project reported that overall, 6.1 million
Americans were unable to vote because of felony disenfranchisement. Currently, because of the Byzantine rules, an estimated
3.1 million people who have completed their sentences are
disenfranchised.

A *Miami Herald* reporter called Florida "the national champion of voter disenfranchisement" in 2016. At the time, 1.7 million people in the Sunshine State had lost their right to vote
because of felony convictions. The state led the way in racializing
felony disenfranchisement as well. "Nearly one-third of those
who have lost the right to vote for life in Florida are black,"
reported the Brennan Center for Justice that same year, "although
African Americans make up just 16 percent of the state's population. Florida's law disenfranchises 21 percent of its total African
American voting-age population."

• • •

The push to eliminate blacks' access to the ballot box dates back to the end of the Civil War. As white Southern leaders strained to maintain their power and curtail the potential strength of the newly freed, Florida wrote felony disenfranchisement into its new constitution. Then the state, like others in the old Confederacy, deployed the burgeoning criminal justice system to craft laws designed for or enforced only against black people. The criminalization of blackness led to labor camps, with the added bonus of the curtailment of blacks' constitutional rights, including voting.

Until Florida's voters said yes to an amendment to their state constitution in November 2018, Florida was one of only four states, including Kentucky, Iowa, and Virginia, that "permanently" disenfranchised felons. The term "permanent" means that there is no automatic restoration of voting rights. Instead, there is a process to plead for dispensation, which usually requires petitioning all the way up to the governor after a specified waiting period.

Florida's Republican governor Rick Scott made that task doubly difficult. The Florida Office of Executive Clemency, which he led, met only four times a year and had more than ten thousand applications waiting to be heard. An ex-offender couldn't even apply to have his or her voting rights restored until five to seven years after all the sentencing requirements were met. The process is therefore daunting enough as it is, but Scott slowed it down considerably. His predecessor, a moderate Republican turned Democrat, "restored rights to 155,315 ex-offenders" over a four-year span, reported the *Miami Herald* in 2016.

Between 2011 and 2016 Scott had approved only 2,340 cases. Equally unsettling, a study by the *Palm Beach Post* found that he had restored the voting rights to twice as many Republicans as Democrats and that black people "accounted for a lower percentage of restorations under Scott than under any of his predecessors, Republican or Democrat, going back at least half a century."

The Department of Justice has exacerbated the threat. In July 2017, its Civil Rights Division sent a letter to forty-four states demanding details on "how they keep their voter rolls up-to-date," reported the Brennan Center for Justice. There was nothing in the letter at all inquiring about what the states were doing, via the NVRA, to expand access to the ballot box. Rather, using language that echoed that of Kris Kobach, Jon Husted, Brian Kemp, J. Christian Adams, and every other vote suppressor in power, Attorney General Jeff Sessions focused on "voter roll maintenance," which has been the key to purging millions of American citizens from the voter rolls. The seeming legality of hiding behind the language of the "integrity of the ballot box" and merely following the mandate of the NVRA for "voter roll maintenance," all the while gutting the Fifteenth Amendment, is why purging voter rolls is really "undercover racism."

The United States is now at the tipping point where the concerted efforts at the state and federal level to purge American citizens from voter rolls and cull and homogenize the electorate is a clear and present danger to democracy.

★ PART FOUR ★

RIGGING THE RULES

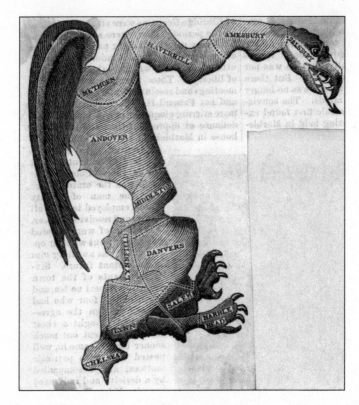

Based on the reconfiguration of Massachusetts districts in an 1810 election, this cartoon is the origin of the term "gerrymander."

15

ELBRIDGE GERRY'S
SALAMANDER

IN 2016, THE ECONOMIST INTELLIGENCE UNIT, A
British outfit, which had evaluated 167 nations on sixty different
indicators, reported that the United States had slipped into the
category of a "flawed democracy."

Similarly, the Electoral Integrity Project, based at the University of Sydney in Australia and at Harvard University in the
United States, using a number of benchmarks and measurements, was stunned to find that when it applied those same calculations in the United States as it had in Cuba, Indonesia, and
Sierra Leone, North Carolina was "no longer considered to be a
fully functioning democracy." Indeed, if it were an independent
nation, North Carolina would rank somewhere between Iran
and Venezuela. The basic problem in North Carolina was that,
despite the overt performance of ballots, precincts, and vote

tallies, legislators and congressional representatives were actually *selected* for office rather than elected.

The deft art of gerrymandering—the deliberate altering of a locality's boundaries in a way that favors one political party or group—is key to understanding the decline of democracy in America.

It wasn't supposed to be that way. The US Constitution requires that legislative boundaries be redrawn every decade after the Census to align and realign congressional representatives with population shifts and changes.

From the very beginning, however, chicanery was afoot.

In 1788, Revolutionary War hero Patrick Henry recognized that whoever drew those legislative district lines could reward friends with political power and simultaneously banish enemies into the electoral wilderness. And he was keen on keeping his nemesis James Madison out of Congress.

So Patrick Henry convinced the Virginia legislature to manipulate the boundaries of his enemy's district so that the election eventually pitted Madison against the revered James Monroe for the coveted seat.

In 1810, when Massachusetts governor Elbridge Gerry drew a district in the shape of a salamander to corral his rivals and neutralize their influence, the term "gerrymander" became a descriptive and ongoing part of the American political lexicon and life. Gerrymandering became so pervasive and disruptive that in 1891 President Benjamin Harrison called it nothing but "political robbery."

Two distinct types of gerrymandering emerged on the American landscape.

One was racial.

The other partisan.

Both were lethal.

Racial gerrymandering is designed to create an all-white power structure virtually impervious to the rights, claims, and public policy needs of people of color. Especially after the passage of the 1965 Voting Rights Act, the courts took the circuitous path of trying to ensure that people of color had the chance to elect representatives whose interest aligned with theirs while guarding against the "packing" of blacks or Latinos in one or two isolated districts, which meant those congressional representatives were mere tokens who would have little influence in the larger halls of power.

Partisan gerrymandering seeks to ensconce in power, regardless of the vote count, a particular party's candidates while keeping the competition (and his or her constituents) from having any real say in the development and implementation of laws and public policy.

Thus, regardless of whether it's all white or all one party, the ultimate goal of gerrymandering is to nullify the effect of a democracy.

Beginning in the 1960s, the Civil Rights Movement's call for moral clarity and legal equality finally began to disrupt business as usual. The NAACP, the Student Nonviolent Coordinating Committee, and the Congress of Racial Equality were demanding the full array of black Americans' citizenship rights. Their activism in the courts and the streets had put the all-white, one-party Democratic South under enormous pressure.

Arch-segregationists, however, were not going to give up without a fight.

One of the ways they fought progress was by culling those white politicians who were a bit too liberal.

Voters had already turned their backs on Mississippi governor J. P. Coleman because, although he was an avowed segregationist, he had the audacity to believe that the lynchers who dragged a black man out of jail, beat and chained him, then threw him into the river, should actually be prosecuted. For many white people, Coleman's position was heresy bordering on blasphemy.

Coleman was pilloried by two-time gubernatorial loser Ross Barnett. During the 1959 primary and 1960 general election, "white supremacy was virtually Mr. Barnett's sole campaign theme," the *New York Times* later reported. In 1960, Barnett did not become a three-time loser. He ran unopposed in the general election and became governor.

Congressman Frank Smith also had to go. When he was initially elected in 1951 to Mississippi's third US congressional district, Smith had flown under the racial radar because his credentials for maintaining the status quo appeared unassailable. His father had been killed by a black man and he was from the Delta, one of the most entrenched, racially stratified, violent, and treacherous places in Mississippi. As far as arch-segregationists were concerned, Frank Smith was one of them.

Only he wasn't.

Frank Smith believed in and supported the Civil Rights Movement. There was simply no space in Mississippi's Democratic Party for someone like him. The results of the 1960 Census and the mandatory reapportionment, where Mississippi lost one of its congressional seats, provided the mechanism to get rid of Smith.

As political scientist K. C. Morrison described it, "The legislators devised a reapportionment plan that obliterated [Smith's District Three] by consolidating it with the Second District," which placed Smith in 1962 in a head-to-head competition with that district's Jamie Whitten. The "new district," Morrison continued, "had been gerrymandered in such a way that Whitten," who blasted Smith for supporting desegregation, "was guaranteed a victory."

In the same year that Congressman Smith was gerrymandered out of a job, the US Supreme Court issued a landmark ruling in *Baker v. Carr.* This ruling finally began to place restrictions on how state legislatures drew the boundaries for districts.

Baker v. Carr evolved out of the fact that Tennessee had been using a 1901 statute to determine the electoral districts for state and congressional representatives. The law locked in place the political domination of the countryside and ignored that there had been major shifts in population to urban areas like Memphis and Nashville. While the cities were exploding, rural Tennessee was atrophying, but its clout in the legislature was as powerful as ever. By 1960, in fact, "roughly two-thirds of Tennessee's representatives were being elected by one-third of the state's population."

Memphis resident Charles Baker led a group that sued the state, arguing that the 1901 statute was unconstitutional because even at the time of its passage, it "made no apportionment of Representatives and Senators in accordance with the constitutional formula . . . but instead arbitrarily and capriciously apportioned representatives in the Senate and House without reference . . . to any logical or reasonable formula whatever." And, Baker's case continued, the court should recognize that legislative redress was impossible. The legislature was created and sustained by this unconstitutional law, and, thus, those representatives who owed their very positions to maintaining the status quo had no reason to legislate themselves out of a job. The court, Baker's suit continued, was the only viable mechanism to correct this wrong, because Tennessee's adherence to a calcified statute had caused a "debasement of their votes" that denied those who lived in the cities the equal protection of the laws guaranteed to them by the Fourteenth Amendment.

The state's counterargument was simple. This was a "political," not a constitutional, matter. The district court concurred with Tennessee even though the judges recognized that "the evil" of stripping citizens in major population centers of the real weight of their vote "is a serious one which should be corrected without further delay."

While that lower court held that there was no standard and no rationale for judicial intervention, the US Supreme Court disagreed. The High Court maintained that courts did have the authority to weigh in on this issue. The state's action had a negative impact on constitutional rights of American citizens. In using the 1901 statute to draw congressional districts, Tennessee had diluted the votes of some citizens while privileging others. That dilution violated the Fourteenth Amendment's equal protection clause. In its decision, in pointing to the disparity in the weight of votes, the court thus defined "one person, one vote" as the standard benchmark for democracy. This was reaffirmed in two major subsequent decisions in the 1960s.

That seemingly rock-solid constitutional standard came under assault. States looked for ways to circumvent the law using the dominance of party affiliation in determining districts, in part because partisan gerrymandering seemed to bedevil the court. The uncertainty of exactly what it was and what it wasn't, the difficulty in determining when it existed and when it didn't, only egged on the states as they violated "one person, one vote" as shrewdly, cleverly, and ruthlessly as they could.

Maryland Democrats had crafted districts that looked "as if they were drawn by a child experimenting with an Etch-A-Sketch," said a reporter for the *Baltimore Sun*.

Georgia Democrats had managed to eliminate Republican strongholds even as the state gained congressional seats.

Pennsylvania Republicans, egged on by those in the GOP's national leadership, vowed to make what happened in Georgia "look like a picnic."

In Texas, the 1990 Census allowed Democratic representative Martin Frost to spearhead a redistricting process that virtually gerrymandered the Republicans out of power. "For the next decade, Democrats received a substantially larger share of the seats than their share of the popular vote." By 2000, although the Republicans won 50.8 percent of the congressional vote, they only secured thirteen of thirty seats.

In 2002, Texas Republicans staged a virtual coup, a "knee-capping," even, by using state troopers, the Department of Justice, and the Federal Aviation Administration to track down and corral Democratic legislators who had fled into New Mexico and Oklahoma to avoid a special session. With enough of these legislators dragged back to Austin to ensure a quorum, the Republicans redrew the congressional districts to assure GOP dominance well into the future.

What happened in Pennsylvania, however, would finally give the US Supreme Court a chance to rectify the problem. The 2000 Census required the state's congressional delegation to be reduced by two seats. The Republicans, who controlled both houses of the legislature and the governor's office, received marching orders from "prominent national figures in the Republican Party"—House Majority Leader Tom DeLay and Speaker of the House Dennis Hastert—"to adopt a partisan redistricting plan as a punitive measure against Democrats for having enacted pro-Democrat redistricting plans elsewhere." The resulting gerrymandered map was even more effective than what Mississippi had done to Frank Smith in 1962.

Before the redistricting, Pennsylvania's congressional delegation was composed of eleven Republicans and ten Democrats. The Census-driven reduction of two seats did not lead to an eleven-to-eight ratio, however, but one that would yield thirteen or fourteen Republicans out of a total of nineteen seats. This gerrymandered map, this reconfiguration of power that gave inordinate power to mid-Pennsylvania and diluted the political voice of voters in Philadelphia and Pittsburgh, landed the state before the US Supreme Court in 2003 as Democrats sued.

At that point, the ACLU and the Brennan Center for Justice filed an amicus curiae brief, that is, a supporting legal document filed in a case by a party not involved in that case.

They laid out that partisan gerrymandering was a scourge on democracy—that it silenced the will of the people and exchanged it for computer-assisted, carefully drafted maps that entrenched power in the hands of the few.

They hammered on the long history of partisan gerrymandering and how it eroded citizens' confidence in the government, in the meaningfulness of voting, and in democracy.

They warned that to continue down this road would entrench a one-party system in power whose only threat would be challengers from the extremist wing.

They predicted that the craftily created districts would make these so-called representatives absolutely unrepresentative because they would be impervious to the will of voters.

We are creating, they insisted, a system in which "elections do not matter." As long as the system puts in power those who received the least number of votes, American democracy was imperiled.

Four of the justices were not persuaded. Led by Justice Antonin Scalia, they asserted in *Vieth v. Jubelirer* (2004) that partisan gerrymandering was beyond the scope of any judicial scrutiny. It was a political issue and not one where the court could insert itself. There was no standard to determine the difference between plain old gerrymandering and partisan gerrymandering, they ruled. And eighteen years of cases after *Davis v. Bandemer* (1986), where the justices held out the possibility of making that distinction, hadn't brought the Supreme Court any closer to a workable standard.

While Scalia and three others threw up their hands in seeming despair about trying to adjudicate something as legally vague as "fairness," one justice, Anthony Kennedy, held out a flicker of hope that although there was no standard in 2004 that could determine partisan gerrymandering, that might not always be the case. Still, his doubt led to a plurality decision—meaning the decision received the most votes but not more than half— giving a green light to partisan gerrymandering and leaving the states without even the possibility of judicial review.

That decision, combined with the increasing diversity of the cities, the mounting whiteness of the suburbs and rural areas, the rightward shift in the Republican Party, the role of dark money and the *Citizens United* decision in elections, and the rise of powerful computer-mapping software and analytics, created a perfect gerrymandering storm that has not only affected state legislatures but also determined the ideological configuration and policy stances of the US Congress, and, thus, the nation.

As the authors of *Gerrymandering in America* explained, the *Vieth* decision "is not simply a technical decision about whether it is possible to detect political gerrymander. . . . Rather, it strikes at the heart of the right to equal representation that the Supreme Court championed in the 1960s."

The Supreme Court's abdication—just as in *Citizens United* and *Shelby County v. Holder*—unleashed anti-democracy forces across the American political landscape. The ultimate tipping point was after the 2010 midterm elections, when the GOP swept legislative and gubernatorial elections and used that victory to declare war.

Protestors on Wall Street oppose the 2017 tax bill HR 1. Despite public outcry against the bill, it passed anyway—partially because heavily gerrymandered districts offered Republicans protection from losing their seats in upcoming elections.

16

OF THE TEXAS GLOCK, THE GEORGIA FLAT-CAT ROAD KILL, AND OTHER ABERRATIONS

CONTROL OF THE LEGISLATURE AND THE GOVER-
nor's office in twenty-six states, especially after the completion of
the 2010 Census, gave the GOP the authority to draw congressional district boundaries at will. Control of the statehouse also
provided the opportunity to craft a series of voter suppression
laws and jigger the mechanisms determining how, where, when,
and for whom citizens in their state could vote.

The key step was to unleash what Kevin Drum writing for
Mother Jones magazine called "brute force, computer-driven
gerrymandering."

Some Republicans, like those in North Carolina, brought in
their top mapmaker, Tom Hofeller. His "exceptionally smart"

maps transformed a once 7–6 Democratic congressional majority into a "10–3 GOP stronghold."

Similarly, Michigan, Pennsylvania, Texas (which didn't con-
sult with Hofeller), Wisconsin, and other states began to have
districts that looked like contorted yoga positions or Rorschach
tests: the North Carolina Gimpy Leg, the Texas Glock, the Georgia Flat-Cat Road Kill That Became the Squirrel Not Yet Hit by
a Car, and the Texas 27th Bottle Opener.

Hofeller, using powerful mapping software linked to demographic data and trends, was able to wring every last available
GOP district out of a state and do so in a way that provided safe
districts where there could never be a viable challenge from a Democratic candidate. Indeed, after the high-powered gerrymandering,
"more Americans lived in areas with uncontested elections than . . .
before." And when there is a competition, it usually isn't much.
Only 4.9 percent of Americans live in districts where the margin
of difference between the winner and loser is 5 percent or less.

Meanwhile, the GOP "pack[ed] the rival party's voters tightly
into far fewer districts," creating a power "asymmetry." Because
of the disparity between the numerous Republican districts, which
represent more sparsely populated suburbs and rural areas, and
the handful of Democratic districts, which are drawn around
densely populated urban areas, "there is a 20% Republican advantage when both parties have equal votes, and the Democrats would
in some cases need to win almost 60% of the vote to have a fifty-
fifty chance of having a majority of the state's delegation to the
House of Representatives." This deliberate feature in the electoral
system has resulted in the muting or erasure of the political concerns of those who live and vote in the most populous areas. In

2017, Senators John McCain (Republican from Arizona) and Sheldon Whitehouse (Democrat from Rhode Island) recognized this harsh reality for what it is: "wasted votes and silenced voices."

One of the most striking examples of this jarring phenomenon was the passage of the 2017 tax bill, HR 1 (House Resolution 1). Its features, many predict, will be absolutely injurious to middle- and working-class Americans. And a majority of the people had strongly opposed the bill. The media continued to publish poll after poll reflecting this strong opposition. But it was all to no avail. With wealthy donors threatening to cut off campaign contributions unless the tax bill passed and transferred the lion's share of the $1.5 trillion in resources to their lot, the GOP pressed forward. This was relatively easy to do because many Republicans were convinced that their carefully drawn districts provided ample protection from ballot box anger and retribution.

> "Citizens can't just vote the gerrymandering party out of office, because the maps are too heavily skewed. In fact, that's the whole point of extreme partisan gerrymanders: to insulate the legislative majority from the will of the voters."
> —Brennan Center for Justice

In the 2016 election, for example, Democrats running for seats in the House of Representatives received 1.4 million more votes than their opponents, but Republicans secured thirty-three more seats. And those meticulously crafted districts provided another important benefit as well: they inflated the number of

Republican districts and provided an additional sixteen to twenty-six representatives in Congress, which was more than enough to pass the extremely unpopular tax bill.

Despite the judicial distinction between the partisan gerrymandering that Scalia asserted was beyond the pale of the Supreme Court's authority and racial gerrymandering that requires the highest level of judicial review, known as strict scrutiny, partisan gerrymandering is also about race. As US district judges Xavier Rodriguez and Orlando Garcia observed, this seemingly colorblind method of drawing districts is, instead, all about a "party's willingness to use race for partisan advantage."

The demographic composition of the parties almost dictates it. The Pew Research Center notes that in 2016, 86 percent of Republican voters were white, while black people had stayed at 2 percent since 1992. Meanwhile, Democratic voters were much more diverse: 57 percent were white, 21 percent were black, 12 percent were Hispanic, 3 percent were Asian, and 5 percent described themselves as mixed race or "other." The racial demographics of the parties, therefore, carry over into the ways that the district lines are constructed. In Georgia, when two Republican incumbents barely won reelection in 2016 because their platforms did not resonate with the growing black population in the Atlanta suburbs, the GOP-controlled legislature simply redrew their districts, moving the black neighborhoods over to a Democrat and extracting her white constituents to Republican districts.

Just as Mississippi in the 1960s exemplified the contortions a state was willing to undertake to politically silence its sizable minority population, Texas is the poster child for trying to accomplish something similar in the twenty-first century.

The 2010 Census indicated that Texas's population had grown significantly. As a result of its 4.3 million new residents, four additional seats were added to the state's congressional delegation. That growth, however, was the direct result of the Latino and black population increasing by 42 and 22 percent, respectively. "In other words," wrote journalist Robert Draper in his article "The League of Dangerous Mapmakers," "without the minority growth, Texas—now officially a majority-minority state—would not have received a single new district."

The GOP-dominated legislature, nevertheless, set out to produce what Draper called "lavishly brazen maps" where, wrote another journalist, "white Republicans were awarded three of the four new seats that resulted from Democratic-leaning minority population growth." In the Lone Star State, whites are 45 percent of the state's population but control 70 percent of the congressional districts. This disparity is even more obvious in the Dallas–Fort Worth area, where whites are only 20 percent of the population but have 80 percent of the congressional seats. As an editorial in the *Dallas Morning News* explained, "Current voting maps erode minority voters' right to choose who they want to represent them—and threaten our democracy more broadly." The state has, therefore, faced a number of lawsuits and has had to go back and redraw, redraw, and redraw again.

Yet it is Wisconsin, one of the most segregated states in the nation, that has become the major legal battlefield over the issue of partisan gerrymandering.

Bill Whitford, lead plaintiff in *Gill v. Whitford*, the case that protested partisan gerrymandering, speaks outside of the Supreme Court.

17

GILL V. WHITFORD

AFTER GAINING CONTROL OF THE WISCONSIN LEG-
islature in the 2010 election, the GOP set out to "create," wrote
the Brennan Center for Justice's Thomas Wolf, "a map for
state assembly elections that would guarantee them large legislative majorities even with a minority of the statewide vote." A
handful of Republican legislators and aides virtually sequestered
themselves in a hotel room and worked diligently over the course
of four months to, wrote Wolf, "engineer maps with the aid of
sophisticated" social science statistical techniques. During this
process, the mapmakers excluded all Democrats from participation and "even rank-and-file Republicans were largely left in the
dark, shown only information relating to their specific districts
and only after signing nondisclosure agreements."

When put to the test, the redistricting exceeded the Wisconsin GOP's expectations. In the 2012 election, although Obama
carried the state by seven points and Democrats received more

than 50 percent of the vote, they garnered only 39 percent of the seats in the general assembly. Each subsequent election yielded an increasing number of Republican seats that was decidedly disproportionate to the votes GOP candidates received.

The *Vieth* decision seemed to indicate that there was nothing—no force, no authority—that could stop this. Enter retired law professor Bill Whitford.

Bill Whitford had been meeting with a group in a Madison tea shop regularly, talking politics and believing that extreme partisan gerrymandering was dangerous to democracy. Once this group learned that teams of social scientists had been working on ways to actually measure extreme partisan gerrymandering, the small opening that Justice Kennedy had left in *Vieth* provided the window that Whitford, a dozen Democratic voters, and their team of lawyers needed. They filed suit.

Wisconsin's defense was simple. The state claimed that it had done nothing wrong. It was just politics, and *Vieth* made clear that there was no role for the court in politics. Moreover, if Democrats had fewer districts, it was only because their voters tended to be concentrated in the cities. The districts were drawn based on political geography, the state contended, nothing more. Whitford's lawyers, however, countered that American citizens' right to equal protection under the law had taken a beating because of the state's extreme partisan gerrymandering. The trail of inequality was easily discernible, from the sixty out of ninety-nine seats the GOP won in 2012 to the sixty-three out of ninety-nine in 2014, with nothing approaching that kind of dominance at the ballot box. Democratic voters had been meticulously, ruthlessly, and unconstitutionally undercut and silenced. And while the Supreme Court had earlier ruled that no one could expect proportional representation (for example, that 48 percent of the population should receive 48 percent of the representatives), what was happening in Wisconsin was not about proportional representation. It was about representation, period.

Then, Whitford's team addressed Kennedy's concern and not only provided a way to measure partisan gerrymandering to determine whether it was extreme, but also laid out the standards that could separate egregious cases from traditional redistricting. This meant the courts would not be inundated with frivolous lawsuits.

Law professor Nicholas Stephanopoulos and political scientist Eric McGhee had developed a mathematical formula to assess districting maps. They had looked at geography to see whether the concentration of likely Democratic voters in the cities accounted for the vast seat differential, as Wisconsin had contended. But as they ran their equations and various models, it was apparent that the seats flipped too rapidly from Democratic to Republican for geography to be the driving force. The key, instead, was the maps crafted in that locked room and the "efficiency gap" they created. Wasted votes are the critical element in this equation—whether they are in districts that are so uncompetitive that the winners garnered 94 percent of the vote, as has happened in several Wisconsin elections, or in other districts where voting for a candidate who has absolutely no chance of winning is a vote that has gone for absolute naught. A "gerrymander," the research team explained, "is simply a district plan that results in one party wasting many more votes than its adversary."

Losers are to be expected, of course. It is the structure deter-mining the full extent of that loss that is under scrutiny. Stepha-nopoulos and McGhee have determined that "an efficiency gap larger than 7% may show that one party holds an unconstitu-tional 'systemic advantage' over the other." For example, between the 1970s and 1990s, Republicans averaged a 1.5 percent effi-ciency gap in their favor. Yet, "in the three elections since 2010, that figure rose to 12.3%." In other words, when a majority of the votes garners only 39 percent of the seats in the state assem-bly, those wasted votes are like the canary in the mine signaling that something toxic may be happening down in the shaft. The efficiency gap is, however, only one component. Other tests must be used in conjunction with it to verify those findings.

First, is there a *durable partisan effect*, such as Wisconsin under-going three elections in which the Republicans' vote gains were not overwhelming but their share of the number of seats in the General Assembly continued to grow.

The next part of the standard is *intent* to seek a partisan edge. When that group of Wisconsin Republicans worked away at the maps for four months, excluded every Democrat from the pro-cess, and required nondisclosure agreements from their Republi-can colleagues before they could be shown their own districts, intent had been more than established. To be clear, unitary party control of the government apparatus—both houses of the legisla-ture and the governor's office—is usually an essential condition of intent.

Finally, if the *districts do not meet previous constitutional standards*, such as being compact, contiguous, and within established politi-cal subdivisions, but instead begin to take on the shape of a bug splattered against a windshield or are joined together only during low tide, something could be awry. None of these alone will suffice, but combined they spell out democracy's SOS.

The district court weighed the evidence, assessed the arguments, evaluated the efficiency gap's reliability and validity, and parsed through the other standards and how they strengthened the judiciary's ability to determine whether partisan gerrymandering was in operation. Then the court, in a 2–1 decision, found that Wisconsin had violated American citizens' Fourteenth Amendment rights. With that, partisan gerrymandering was back in the judicial crosshairs. Kennedy's opening in *Vieth* appeared to be just what democracy needed.

Wisconsin appealed, and the arguments before the US Supreme Court set off judicial fireworks.

Trump appointee Neil Gorsuch showed his contempt for the efficiency gap's methodology. He mocked the "standard" as being no more than a "touch" of this and a "touch" of that, "a pinch of this, a pinch of that," as if it were his "steak rub" and "not a real set of criteria." He questioned whether the court had any business meddling in a state's political affairs. There seemed, to him, no constitutional reason for this case to exist.

As Gorsuch harangued Whitford's attorney on this point, Justice Ruth Bader Ginsburg had had just about enough and asked a basic question that any first-year law student should know the answer to: What is the basis for "one person, one vote"?

As Whitford's lawyer, Paul M. Smith, recited previous Supreme Court decisions in *Baker v. Carr*, *Reynolds v. Sims*, and others, Ginsburg's pointed query sent a powerful signal. Later she cut to the core of the issue: "The precious right to vote" was "what's really behind all of this . . . if you can stack a legislature in this way, what incentive is there for a voter to exercise his vote? . . . What becomes of the precious right to vote?"

That wasn't an issue for Chief Justice Roberts. He derided the "efficiency gap" as "gobbledygook," "a bunch of baloney." Roberts insisted that what Whitford and the Democrats wanted was "proportional representation, which has never been accepted as a political principle in the history of this country."

Smith countered brilliantly that this was about symmetry. If in one election, party A received 54 percent of the vote and received 58 percent of the seats, then the same should hold true when party B wins 54 percent of the vote. "That's symmetry." But, Smith continued, what Wisconsin's GOP did was to spend "those four months in that locked room doing two things, trying to maximize the amount of bias and eliminating . . . competitive districts." Where there had been twenty of those districts, the Republicans had reduced that number to ten and "tinkered with it and tinkered with it to make sure that even of that 10, they thought they could get at least seven. They ended up getting eight and then eventually all 10."

Justice Stephen Breyer proffered an approach to see if there was a way of simplifying "all of that social science stuff and the computer stuff . . . to something manageable." Something that the courts could use. In four steps he laid it out. First, "was there one-party control of the redistricting"? Second, "is there partisan asymmetry? In other words, does the map treat the political parties differently? . . . Good evidence of that," Breyer added, "is a party that got 48 percent of the vote got a majority of the legislature." Third, "is there going to be persistent asymmetry over a range of votes?" Wisconsin's 2012, 2014, and 2016 elections "shows you that," he said. And fourth, was there any "justification," any "motive," for crafting a districting map that is one of "the worst in the country"? As Breyer admired his handiwork, he concluded, "Now, I suspect that that's manageable."

Kennedy asked deep questions about the efficiency gap and how it could reliably identify extreme partisan gerrymandering. Wisconsin's attorney tried to counter that a formula based on hypothetical social science models would drag election decisions out of the political realm where they belonged and place that decision-making in the hands of the federal courts.

Justice Elena Kagan cut him off. There was nothing "hypothetical, airy-fairy, we guess, and then we guess again" happening in this case, she said. "This is pretty scientific by this point."

Justice Sonia Sotomayor then picked up from there. When the GOP used social science methods to devise maps, the group in the locked hotel room ran enough models to know that the first one would not yield the results they wanted. "Your map drawer . . . started out with the Court plan, they created three or four different maps, they weren't partisan enough. They created three or four more maps, they weren't partisan enough. And they finally got to the final map, after maybe 10 different tries of making it more partisan, and they achieved a map that was the most partisan. . . . And it worked. It worked better than they even expected. . . . So, if it's the most extreme map they could make, why isn't that enough to prove partisan asymmetry and unconstitutional gerrymandering?"

As Wisconsin's attorney tried to answer but fumbled badly, Sotomayor circled around again. They "kept going back to fix the map to make it more gerrymandered," she noted. "That's undisputed. People involved in the process had traditional maps that complied with traditional criteria and then went back and threw out those maps and created more—some that were more partisan. . . . So why didn't they take one of the earlier maps?" The answer, the confession, in fact, explained everything. "Because there was no constitutional requirement that they do so."

Through the oral arguments, it became clear. Conservatives on the bench had dug in behind Scalia's claim in *Vieth* that partisan gerrymandering was not justiciable. It would sully the court to insert itself in the political process. Meanwhile, the liberals on the bench were greatly concerned about how absolute power had corrupted the democratic process absolutely.

With the GOP takeover, Ginsburg had cut to the core of the issue: What happened to "the precious right to vote"?

Sotomayor was just as concerned: "It's okay to stack the decks so . . . even though it [one party] gets a minority of votes . . . [it] can get the majority of seats?" She was compelled to ask, "Could you tell me what the value is to democracy from political gerrymandering? . . . How does that help our system of government?"

Gerrymandering's pernicious, corrosive effects on democracy and our system of government are well understood and documented. Whoever controls redistricting controls Congress. Gerrymandering has a horrific effect on voter behavior. Those in competitive districts are more likely to vote. Those in safe, uncompetitive districts stay home more often on Election Day. Just as Ginsburg surmised, there appears to be no "incentive" to vote. Moreover, that "redistricting dampens turnout in the subsequent election cycle, especially among black registrants." The import for what this means to Democratic candidates is profound. "The drop in overall turnout among [black Americans] attributed to redistricting can produce sizable electoral effects." As expected, black voter turnout declined in every gerrymandered swing state during the 2016 election.

The damage to democracy is exacerbated by this feature of partisan gerrymandering: there are deliberately fewer competitive districts. No surprise, then, in the 2016 election, 97 percent of US House of Representatives incumbents won reelection.

In 2019, Chief Justice Roberts wrote for the majority in the partisan or political gerrymandering case *Rucho v. Common Cause*: "We conclude that partisan gerrymandering claims present political questions beyond the reach of the federal courts."

Justice Kagan disagreed that the federal courts had no role to play in these cases. In her dissent, she wrote, "Of all times to abandon the Court's duty to declare the law, this was not the one."

The lack of accountability to the public, therefore, creates another vicious dynamic. There's the inflexibility inherent in one-party rule. Then there's the internal party catalyst pushing the agenda further and further to the extreme in order for challengers to differentiate themselves from what is now orthodoxy. It creates a hardening in legislative positions that requires those in power to refuse to compromise or seek solutions across the political aisle for fear of running into a modern-day Ross Barnett, where even the most commonsensical stance (for example, that lynchers should be brought to justice) becomes inflammatory and politically untenable.

Voters in line for the 2016 presidential election in Christmas, Florida.

18

MORE DIRTY TRICKS

UNFORTUNATELY, THE ASSAULT ON DEMOCRACY IS not only about the way congressional and legislative district lines are drawn. The undermining of democracy is also achieved in the way long, seemingly interminable lines at the voting booth have been artificially created.

Reported *Mother Jones* magazine of the long lines in Maricopa County, Arizona, in the 2016 primary election: "The last person to cast a ballot didn't do so until after midnight, according to the *Arizona Republic*, nearly five hours after the Democratic race had already been called for Hillary Clinton, and a few hours after Donald Trump was declared as the Republican winner."

Those lines, and so many others just like them, take their toll. In their article "Waiting to Vote," two distinguished political scientists asserted that long lines "discourage voting, lower voter confidence, and impose economic costs on voters." What's more, just as voting is "habit-forming," not voting is as well. Once discouraged, it becomes a difficult pattern to break.

As endemic as long lines have become, they are not a fixture in most communities. The conditions that bring about five-hour wait times, or thousands standing in line, or only forty people able to get through and cast their ballots after three hours, are concentrated overwhelmingly in minority precincts.

In 2012, on average, black people had to wait in line twice as long as white people to vote. In the "10 Florida precincts with the longest delays . . . almost 70 percent of voters were Latino or black." Nationwide, in the 2012 election, whites who lived in white neighborhoods had the shortest wait times of all citizens— just seven minutes. Behind the lines, beneath the sometimes hours of waiting, is a deliberate and cruel hoax played on millions of citizens. Minority neighborhoods, despite their population density, have been allocated significantly fewer resources by election officials.

Fewer poll workers.

Fewer operable machines.

And fewer opportunities to vote, as Republican legislatures, such as those in Ohio, Indiana, Florida, and North Carolina, have slashed the days and times available for early voting. Early voting had, in previous elections, been one of the key ways to take the economic burden off a generally working-class population that had been forced to choose between voting on Tuesday and missing hours at the job, or going to work and not participating in electing the officials and policies that affect one's life. Latinos, for example, are the least likely racial or ethnic group to vote in person on Election Day.

In 2008, before Florida reduced early voting, black Americans were 13 percent of the electorate but more than 35 percent of those who voted before Election Day. The conscious decision of election officials to shortchange Latino and black neighborhoods' access to the polls, to place older, barely working, and, in the case of Detroit in 2016, nonworking machines at their precincts wreaks havoc on democracy.

In Ohio, for example, the secretary of state allocates only one polling station per county for early voting.

Fair?

Absolutely not.

Because all counties are not equal.

Take Pickaway County: it has fewer than sixty thousand residents total.

Take Hamilton County, where Cincinnati is located: it has a population of more than *eight hundred thousand*. Yet despite this seismic disparity, each had only one early voting polling place available.

There were, obviously, no lines in Pickaway County. Hamilton County, however, in trying to squeeze a population of that magnitude through only one facility, had a line that stretched a quarter mile.

This electoral resource distribution policy uses geography as a proxy for race and puts a distinct burden on voters who live in major urban areas in the state—Cleveland, Columbus, Cincinnati, and Dayton among them—and, therefore, disadvantages blacks. Whereas Pickaway County, for example, has only 1,881 black Americans, Franklin County, where Columbus is located, has more than 274,000 black American residents. The allocation of one early voting spot, especially for a population whose median income is a little more than thirty-one thousand dollars (a full twenty thousand dollars below the state median), is designed to corrosively and subtly lower black voter turnout. When pressed to account for a policy that could have this kind of deleterious impact, the chairman of the Franklin County Republican Party explained, "I guess I really actually feel we shouldn't contort the voting process to accommodate the urban—read African American—voter turnout machine."

Other ploys to strip election resources from people-of-color communities abound. By the time the 2016 election was held, for example, there were 868 fewer polling places available in previous VRA preclearance counties. Scholars have found that "moving a polling place can affect"—and not for the better—"the decision to vote."

North Carolina, in what MSNBC reporter Zachary Roth called a "subtler maneuver" than gerrymandering and voter ID laws, "moved the location of almost one-third of the state's early voting sites" in 2014. The moves, wrote Roth in 2015, "will significantly increase the distance African Americans have to travel to vote early, while leaving white voters largely unaffected."

This was deliberate.

An earlier study indicated that for every one-tenth of a mile increase to a polling place, voting by registered voters declines by 0.5 percent. The ratio in that study suggests that "North Carolina's changes might have kept nearly 19,000 black voters from the polls."

In Macon, Georgia, election officials moved the new polling station for the black precinct to the sheriff's office.

In Sparta, Georgia, a consolidation of polls left the one assigned to the majority black neighborhood seventeen miles away.

Only heightened vigilance and major protests in both cases corrected those moves.

In Florida and Texas, the legislatures changed the laws to make voter registration drives or assistance "a risky business" by requiring months of courses or sworn oaths under the penalty of felony criminal prosecution, short and unreasonable turnaround times to submit registration cards to election authorities, and unnatural county barriers on registration activities that ignored the growth of multicounty metropolises.

The result in Florida was that the League of Women Voters, which had led voter registration drives for seven decades, ceased operations, pulled out of the state, and sued.

In Texas, voter registration is so onerous, criminalized even, that there are more unregistered voters there than the total population of twenty states.

Texas and Georgia have also interpreted laws about "assisting" at the polls to ensnare a young Indian man helping his Bengali-speaking mother translate a ballot, and a black second-generation civil rights warrior in southern Georgia, who, when asked, simply showed a young woman how to use the voting machine. Both the son and the black doyenne then faced felony charges, which, by design, sent a strong warning signal to both their communities.

In short, rigging the rules to suppress or dilute the vote of millions of citizens to affect the outcome of an election has come almost naturally to many of these politicians and public officials. Adjusting lines here and there has demonstrated the high-tech wizardry of gerrymandering and the low-tech, traditional means of starving minority communities of resources necessary to participate fully in American democracy.

Yet, none of this has gone unchallenged. The numerous lawsuits, the protests, the op-eds, the investigative journalists digging into the arcane minutiae of electoral law and legislative intent, all indicate that the light cannot be snuffed out.

> "When voter suppression still exists and when we have to stand up for what we believe in and what is right, we will do it."
>
> —Gwen Westbrooks of Macon, Georgia, who helped organize the successful resistance to a plan to move a polling station in a majority-black neighborhood to the sheriff's office shortly before the 2016 election

★ PART FIVE ★

THE RESISTANCE

Future US House representative John Lewis (right) leads marchers across Edmund Pettus Bridge from Selma, Alabama, to Montgomery, Alabama's state capital, on March 7, 1965.

19

SWEET HOME ALABAMA?

MAY 14, 1961, NEAR ANNISTON, ALABAMA: A FIRE-
bombed Greyhound bus, listing to one side, its tires shredded,
doors jammed shut, and Molotov cocktails sending terror,
screams, and thick black smoke pouring out its windows. Freedom riders gingerly pick broken teeth out of their blood-soaked
mouths.

Spring 1963, in Birmingham, Alabama: Firehoses slam black
bodies against brick walls and hurl nonviolent protesters, often
children, down the street. Snarling, fangs-bared German shep-
herds in the service of law enforcement strain to rip open the
flesh of unarmed black people.

September 15, 1963, in Birmingham, Alabama: Stretchers
emerge from a bombed-out church with white sheets draped over
the lifeless bodies of four little girls.

March 7, 1965, in Selma, Alabama: State police and

horseback-mounted sheriff's deputies trample, teargas, and whip men, women, and children on the Edmund Pettus Bridge.

The consequences of that brutality, of that way of governing, have permeated Alabama well into the twenty-first century. Although the form of oppression is much subtler, it is equally devastating.

In 2017, the United Nations Special Rapporteur on Extreme Poverty and Human Rights found pools of sewage in the woods behind homes in parts of the state's Black Belt counties because there is no waste-disposal infrastructure and the government refused to build any. Back in 2011, a UN report stated that the "Alabama Department of Public Health estimates that the number of households in Lowndes County with inadequate or no septic systems range from 40 to 90 per cent; it has reported that 50 per cent of the conventional, onsite septic systems are currently failing or are expected to fail in the future." As a result, fecal-contaminated water has made *E. coli* and hookworm, indicative of extreme systemic poverty, prevalent throughout the Black Belt counties.

In 2017, Alabama was next to last in infant health. A journalist reported that the "death rate for African American infants is more than two times higher than the rate for white infants." She called that statistic "a stubborn trend that has persisted for the last several years."

Alabama is also ranked forty-seventh in education, forty-eighth in economic opportunity, and forty-fourth in unemployment.

This is the toxic bouillabaisse that gave rise to Judge Roy Moore as the Republican candidate for the US Senate in a 2017 special election needed to fill the vacancy left when President

Trump tapped Alabama's senator Jeff Sessions for the job of US attorney general.

Roy Moore had been a reckless military police officer during the Vietnam War. Similarly, he was a mediocre law student.

He was also an Alabama Supreme Court chief justice who had to be removed twice from the bench because he openly and proudly flouted and defied the US Constitution.

He publicly questioned whether women were qualified to hold elected office.

He was a gay-bashing, Islam-hating, "conservative extremist" (in the words of David Corn with *Mother Jones* magazine) who thought the last time America was truly great was during slavery. "I think it was great at the time," he said days before the special election, "when families were united—even though we had slavery—they cared for one another. . . . Our families were strong, our country had a direction."

After the 2017 Republican primary, this was the man poised to be the next US senator from Alabama.

Republicans had won every US Senate election in Alabama over the previous twenty-five years. What's more, since the US Supreme Court's 2013 decision in *Shelby County v. Holder*, the state had amassed a powerful array of voter suppression techniques and laws targeted at the one constituency that could possibly give Doug Jones, Moore's white Democratic opponent, something beyond a "sliver of hope" of winning.

Alabama's voting laws favored Republican US Senate candidate Roy Moore in a 2017 special election.

20

OF ABORIGINES
AND ILLITERATES

ONCE ALABAMA WAS FREED FROM THE OVERSIGHT of the VRA and preclearance, every twist and turn of the assault on voting rights was mobilized to go after black and poor folk, which the state had in abundance.

A 2017 study showed that fourteen of Alabama's seventeen Black Belt counties had "a poverty rate higher than 25 percent," reported Anna Claire Vollers. Moreover, only the Black Belt counties had that distinction. And, at the sites of historic voting rights battles—Dallas County, Lowndes County, and Perry County—the poverty rate ranged from 34.6 percent to 40 percent. As if Alabama's impoverished people didn't have it hard enough, the state created an additional series of hurdles to get to the ballot box.

Each redrawn boundary, each closed polling place, each

understaffed, barely equipped polling station, each long line, and each ID requirement all took a toll on voter turnout.

The first test was the 2014 midterm election when the state's voter ID law went into effect. As Sherrilyn Ifill noted, "Alabama voter turnout reached a shameful nadir, plummeting to the lowest it had been in decades." In counties with sizable populations of people of color, Alabama achieved what no other state had: a full 5 percent decline in voter turnout.

The road to this "shameful nadir" began even before the 2013 *Shelby County v. Holder* decision that gutted the VRA. Two years before it, in 2011, the Alabama legislature rushed through a voter ID law that disqualified utility bills, bank statements, and other documents as viable proofs of residency and instead required government-issued photo IDs to cast a ballot. Republican lawmakers had actually recorded themselves discussing how to "depress the turnout of black voters—whom they called 'aborigines' and 'illiterates' " in the 2010 midterm election, wrote Scott Douglas, executive director of the Greater Birmingham Ministries, in a 2017 *New York Times* op-ed. The law was so intentionally racist—it would never have passed the VRA's litmus test—that the state didn't even bother to send it up to the DOJ for preclearance as the VRA required. The bill lay dormant until the *Shelby* decision was handed down.

Alabama's new voter ID law went into effect in June 2014.

Problem #1: Government-issued photo ID for those living in public housing was not an acceptable voter ID. This in a state where black Americans made up 71 percent of its public housing residents.

Problem #2: Yes, people could get a voter ID at the

Department of Motor Vehicles, but then Governor Robert Bentley tried to close the DMV locations in the six counties where black people made up more than 70 percent of the population, and he shuttered the DMVs in another eleven counties where blacks made up more than half of the residents. The impact would be devastating. A Brennan Center for Justice report, in fact, showed that "almost a third of Alabama's voting-age population lived more than 10 miles away from the nearest license-issuing office that was open more than two days per week."

The state tried to pretend that its alternate-ID mobile unit would supplant the brick-and-mortar sites, but, by design, it didn't even come close. Alabama issued only 5,070 voter cards of the quarter million its own calculations estimated were actually needed. At one point, the link on the secretary of state's website "directing voters to places where they could get a free ID led to a blank page." Kathleen Unger, the president and CEO of VoteRiders, which assists citizens in getting the ID they need to vote, saw this as a typical move. "The lack of clear information, frankly, . . . the lack of correct information or internally consistent information online. . . . It's a big problem. . . . Sadly," Unger concluded, "I am not surprised."

Despite the attempted closing of the DMVs in the Black Belt counties, the demonstrated inadequacy of the mobile units, and the lack of information on the secretary of state's website, Alabama, nonetheless, claimed that its online registration would solve the problem. However, 56 percent of those living in Alabama's rural counties, including the Black Belt, did not have access to the internet. Neither did 20 percent of those in urban areas.

Another possibility was to physically travel to another county to get a driver's license, but "13.8 percent of Black households in Alabama as compared to 4 percent of white households . . . have no access to a vehicle." For those without a car, public transportation was the only viable means to get the card required to vote. But Alabama "invests no state money in public transportation," Sherrilyn Ifill pointed out to Governor Bentley in 2015, and was ranked forty-eighth in the nation in "intercity transit access" for 844,000 rural residents.

There was still, supposedly, one more option: the local courthouse. Secretary of State John Merrill praised this opportunity where "anybody can go any day of the week—as long as the courthouse is open—and apply for a voter ID." But as one journalist pointed out, "Since 2013, many Alabama courthouses have been operating on reduced hours, due to budget cuts."

Added to that was the issue of treating the local courthouse—a central component of a notorious criminal justice system—as a viable, race-neutral space to obtain a voter ID card. This despite the fact that the prison population was 54 percent black although black people are only 26 percent of the population and where more than half of those on death row in the state are black people.

For John Merrill and other Republican lawmakers, the hoops people had to go through to get a voter ID were not a problem. The problem, said Merrill, was the people. "If you're too sorry or lazy to get up off of your rear and to go register to vote, or to register electronically, and then to go vote, then you don't deserve that privilege," he said in a 2016 interview.

Note that he called voting a "privilege" and not a right.

"As long as I'm secretary of state of Alabama," Merrill boasted, "you're going to have to show some initiative to become a registered voter in this state."

Alabama was, in other words, going to continue to make the right to vote an obstacle course, creating more hurdles and trenches to jump over and walls to climb. Thus, although, as *Facing South* reported, the state's population grew by "nearly 2 percent from 2010 to 2016," Alabama closed down "almost 7 percent" of its precincts. And, as noted previously, because of *Shelby County v. Holder*, by 2016, there were 868 fewer precincts in Section 5 jurisdictions. Sixty-six of those were in Alabama alone.

As if that weren't enough, by August 2017 Merrill purged the voter rolls, "putting 340,162 people . . . on inactive voter status." He explained that he was merely "following federal and state law" and had used the established postcard method, where his office mailed a notice that required a response within a limited, defined time or the recipient would be removed as a registered voter and placed in electoral limbo—the inactive roll. That a state representative landed on the inactive roll although she "never got [a postcard] and neither did [her] wife" or that subsequent complaints identified, among others, a woman who had voted in the same precinct since 2005 only to be turned away at the polling station, suggested, as the Southern Poverty Law Center asserted, that "the process used by the secretary of state is deeply flawed." Merrill actually conceded that "many voters might be discouraged from voting, because they don't have time to pursue the matter." And then, he left the issue right there—with discouraged voters and a deeply flawed process.

That sense of confusion, obfuscation, and discouragement eddied right over to the issue of felony disenfranchisement. In 1901, Alabama stripped voting rights from, among others, those convicted of crimes of "moral turpitude." For more than one hundred years, though, the state had refused to lay out what crimes actually fell under that broad definition. In fact, some registrars interpreted it to mean misdemeanors, such as vagrancy, and other charges that law enforcement liked to reserve for black people. By the twenty-first century, 15 percent of black adults in the state were disenfranchised by this 1901 Jim Crow statute specifically designed to limit black voters and, as the US Supreme Court had observed, " 'to establish white supremacy in this State,' " quoting the chairman of the 1901 convention.

After much pressure and further litigation from the ACLU, the NAACP, and other civil rights organizations, in 2017, under HB 282, Alabama crafted a definitive list of crimes that fell under the banner of "moral turpitude": murder, rape, and treason through to certain burglaries and drug trafficking. After the bill passed, there were more than "250,000 otherwise qualified citizens—nearly 8 percent of the population," reported an ACLU attorney, who had previously lost their voting rights but were unaware those rights were now restored. Merrill, nonetheless, did not take any initiative to inform those people.

Finally, in addition to all the other methods of voter suppression, the state had gerrymandered districts that were so obviously racially biased that the federal courts eventually slapped them down. Alabama drew its legislative boundaries to "pack" as many voters of color into as few districts as possible, thus giving disproportionate weight to white voters and, as the research is clear, seeking to demoralize blacks and Latinos so that they wouldn't even bother to vote.

Atlantic magazine reporter Vann R. Newkirk II summed up how intentionally daunting the barricades to voting in 2017 were. "Voting has always been burdensome for black people in Alabama," he noted. There were the standard obstacles of ID, limited polling places, purged voter rolls, and more, which had all been deployed, and meanwhile, the tried-and-true voter modernization techniques were simply not available. Newkirk explained, "Early voting, which has been a key factor for other states in increasing black turnout, is not permitted in Alabama. The state also doesn't have no-fault absentee voting, preregistration for teens, or same-day registration. In all, it's harder to vote in Alabama than just about anywhere else."

Frankly, it looked hopeless. Roy Moore was on the cusp of shaping the laws for the United States of America in the twenty-first century, with a vision that was clearly nineteenth-century antebellum. He had actually said, wrote a CNN reporter, that "getting rid of constitutional amendments after the Tenth Amendment would 'eliminate many problems' in the way the US government is structured." Amendments following the Tenth include the ones ending slavery (Thirteenth), defining citizenship and due process (Fourteenth), guaranteeing the right to vote without racial discrimination (Fifteenth), providing for women's right to vote (Nineteenth), and ending the poll tax (Twenty-Fourth).

With that vision of what would make America great, Roy Moore had the financial backing of the Republican Party and the endorsement of President Donald Trump.

The wing-and-a-prayer consensus was that stopping this avowed bigot from being elected as a US senator would require combining votes from disgusted whites with a black voter turnout rate that surpassed even that for Obama.

One of Moore's legal colleagues added another hard-core reality fact about Red State Alabama. "Southern Baptists control the damn state," he said. "And they'll vote for Roy. It'll be a landslide." Alabamian Devon Crawford, a divinity student at the University of Chicago who came home to vote against the judge, knew exactly what that meant. He told a reporter that Moore's version of Christianity was "really just a masquerade for white supremacy."

Yet there has always been more than one kind of Christianity roiling and churning in Alabama. As Martin Luther King Jr. called upon it in 1963 from a Birmingham jail, so, too, did the Greater Birmingham Ministries and Brown Chapel AME Church in Selma.

Also into the breach stepped historically black colleges and universities, which became key organizing sites for millennials.

There was also the NAACP. With branches spread throughout Alabama, it mounted a fierce ground game.

Other groups, such as the ACLU, the NAACP LDF, The Ordinary People Society (TOPS), and BlackPAC, played key roles in taking on voter suppression and fighting for democracy.

The resistance relied on traditional as well as new media to message key constituencies about the consequences of this election.

The resistance recognized deep political fissures, especially within the ruling party, and had the savvy to communicate the impact of standing on the wrong side of history.

The resistance also tapped into necessary outside funding but knew that the effectiveness of those resources depended on local ownership of the process.

Déjà vu.

In 1963, John Lewis, then the president of the Student Non-violent Coordinating Committee, returned from the March on Washington with SNCC's call for "one man, one vote" ringing in his ears. As civil rights activist Andrew Young stated, however, "We knew enough about the political situation to know you couldn't prepackage a movement." The local "people had a dynamic, and you had to get in and work with those people." They, and only they, knew the lay of the land. They knew who the movers, the shakers, and the fakers were. They knew the strengths and the weaknesses of the place, the people, and the values that had put them in that moment. For the activists in the 1960s, they knew who brought Alabama to its knees, who made the nation listen, and who was responsible for the Voting Rights Act. As Young also recalled: "The local black leadership in Selma was really responsible for the Selma movement."

In 2017, local savvy, determination, and expertise kicked in again—and well before the election. While the media depicted a "last-minute push," this was, in fact, the long game. "Unlike traditional get-out-the-vote campaigns implemented by Democrats in key African American communities close to elections, many of the moving pieces in the Alabama election were funded by entities other than the party or the candidate's campaign, and had been proceeding in stealth for months," reported Vann R. Newkirk. Local activists "had been working to bolster black turnout long before the Senate race gained national attention" because they understood better than anyone else what a tangled, knotted cord the state had woven around voting rights.

It was clear almost immediately how Alabama had withheld, obfuscated, elided, and contradicted so much basic information about eligibility, polling places, and ID availability that confusion could easily create frustration and lead to anemic voter turnout rates. In fact, fewer than 18 percent of eligible citizens had voted in the August 2017 primary. John Merrill, therefore, predicted that the subsequent race between Roy Moore and Doug Jones would have a 25 percent voter turnout rate.

Democracy dies in that kind of darkness.

The Alabama NAACP, working with local churches, the National Pan-Hellenic Council (black fraternities and sororities), the ACLU, and Planned Parenthood held rallies throughout the state to shine a klieg light on all that was at stake. They emphasized that, despite the barriers Alabama threw up to block the people's access to the ballot box, it was essential to "Vote Out Loud!" Hezekiah Jackson, president of the Metro Birmingham NAACP, exclaimed, "We're at a crossroad in the city, in the state, in the country." At stake, continued another speaker, were "healthcare, education and gay rights." Another explained, "For us . . . what's on the ballot is women's rights, human rights, the 1965 Voting Rights [Act]." Benard Simelton, president of the Alabama State Conference of the NAACP, emphasized that "there's things that [you'll] have to lose if you don't get out and vote. Social Security—it's not a guarantee. . . . And health care—it's not a guarantee . . . education—you know, Alabama is—like so many other Southern states, the education system is in shambles." Those issues, Simelton understood, "resonated particularly with

African-American voters." But it was even more than that. There was a foreboding sense that the country was moving backward.

And it had to stop. Stop now. Stop here. And it had to stop with them. Alabama's civil rights activists were clear: "We have to do this for ourselves. . . . No one is going to do this for us."

The state, for example, had had no problem sending out mailers telling citizens they could not vote because of a past conviction, when that was not true. Yet, despite the May 2017 law that finally defined "moral turpitude," John Merrill refused to "spend state resources" to correct the error or clarify the new law. Meanwhile, there was a dangerous double-dare in this manufactured ambiguity: the "Alabama voter registration form requires applicants to swear under penalty of perjury that they are a qualified voter," explained a journalist, "but it does not include a list of crimes that are disqualifying." Merrill, however, said the notion that people would be "scared away from filling out voter applications" since they might be charged with a felony because their conviction was for a crime that actually constituted "moral turpitude" was nothing but a "well-laid excuse by liberal minions from around the world."

The threat of criminal prosecution, however, was not a piece of fiction. Alabama had strung criminal penalties and booby traps all around voting. At nearly the very moment Merrill was mocking the baited trap of "moral turpitude" and perjury, he was wielding a brand-new law that allowed him to go after "674 Alabama citizens who voted both in the 2017 Democratic primary and Republican runoff elections," reported Think Progress on October 25, 2017. Jail, frankly, was how Alabama threatened the poor and people of color for daring to vote—it was how in the 1980s the state imprisoned Julia Wilder and Maggie Bozeman. This was no idle threat.

Therefore, Legal Services Alabama (LSA) and the local ACLU stepped in to do the hard work of citizenship education regarding "moral turpitude" and voting rights. The groups ran ads on both radio and social media spreading the word that the new law provided a chance for convicted felons to get back their right to vote. The key, however, was not just awareness of HB 282 but immediate follow-up with workshops and clinics on getting one's voting rights back.

LSA and the ACLU launched "restoration clinics" in Selma's Brown Chapel AME Church, which in the 1960s had served as a key site for voting rights organizing and as a makeshift hospital for those beaten mercilessly on the Edmund Pettus Bridge on Bloody Sunday. At these restoration clinics, volunteers and legal professionals went painstakingly through people's conviction records to see whether the felonies fell into the disenfranchising categories. If they did not, the next step was a workshop on how to register to vote—what materials and documents were needed, such as birth certificates, and how to attain them. There was also an understanding that traditional forms of identification—a passport, a driver's license—are a class-based phenomenon and that alternate IDs, such as official mugshots, could be used to vote.

Restoration clinics were also held in churches in Birmingham, Dothan, and Mobile, as well as in high-visibility caravans that traveled throughout the state, particularly to economically impoverished areas. These clinics, in churches and on wheels, cut through the miasma of mis- and disinformation that swallowed the voting rights of so many poor and black folk in Alabama.

Not surprisingly, right-wingers slung mud at the restoration initiative. A *Breitbart* headline warned that its enemy number one, billionaire George Soros, had an "Army in Alabama to Register Convicted Felons to Vote Against Roy Moore." There was something close to apoplexy that civil rights activists were "taking advantage" of a new law that clarified "moral turpitude" and that Soros was behind it all, providing funding for the ACLU, the NAACP, and, perhaps worst of all in *Breitbart*'s eyes, the Dothan-based The Ordinary People Society, led by Pastor Kenneth Glasgow, who had once been incarcerated.

After Glasgow emerged from prison for a drug conviction, he "spent three years fighting through the pardon process to have his voting rights restored," explained ACLU attorney Julie Ebenstein. It was only years later that he learned "the state had made a mistake. He should never have been disenfranchised in the first place because his drug charge was not a 'moral turpitude' offense." He knew he wasn't alone, and so he had worked with the ACLU to get HB 282 passed and was now on the second phase of that restoration project. There were so "many felons [who] simply believed they could never regain the franchise." But with the new law, Glasgow said, "I've got people all over the state registering people [to vote] . . . in Tuscaloosa, Birmingham, Montgomery, Enterprise, Dothan, Abbeville, Geneva, Gordon, Bessemer, we have a lot."

One of the most important sites of this work was in the local jails and prisons. State law actually allowed absentee ballots for those incarcerated—as long as they had not been convicted of a crime of "moral turpitude." Glasgow and TOPS members, therefore, fanned out and began voting rights and citizenship education sessions in thirty-two carceral facilities.

One man, Spencer Trawick, had lost his right to vote in 2015 after he was convicted of a felony: third-degree burglary. Sitting with Trawick in Dothan jail, Glasgow informed him that this crime did not fall under the definition of "moral turpitude." A stunned Trawick went to work on the necessary paperwork to register to vote that very day under Glasgow's watchful eye.

> "A lot of people get felonies and they just feel like their whole world's shattered because there's a lot of things that you can't do, but now that they passed that law a lot people are going to run towards it."
>
> —Spencer Trawick in November 2017

Meanwhile, the NAACP organized a campaign to dodge, deflect, and blunt every one of the shots that the state took at citizens' voting rights. Just as during the Civil Rights Movement, it didn't seem to be a fair fight. The state had weapons of mass civic destruction. The resistance appeared to be unarmed. But it actually had a determination that would stun Alabama. There was no other viable choice; the toll that voter suppression had already taken on the nation was all too clear. It had placed in the White House, even according to former CIA director John Brennan, a president who is "unstable, inept, inexperienced, and also unethical." Voter suppression had also resulted in that same unethical man controlling the public policies that affected millions of lives. And it looked as if Alabama was trying to replicate that debacle with Roy Moore.

Doug Jones's US Senate race was bolstered by an outpouring of activism from Alabama's black community.

21

"SELMA, LORD, SELMA"

CIVIL SOCIETY KNEW THAT 2016 WAS A WAKE-UP call. And those who were part of it answered the alarm.

Said journalist Vann R. Newkirk II: "GOP dominance, voter suppression, and the stubborn support for Moore among white voters in the state helped revive the kind of black political entities originally built in the state to grapple with Jim Crow."

Those entities drew upon that history and the lessons learned from the 2016 presidential election. They needed to be more deliberate, more purposeful, more focused, and more vigorous to stop Roy Moore from winning the senate race.

In addition to numerous rallies to spread the word about the special election for the Senate seat and its consequences, the next wave was to make direct one-on-one contact with the state's citizens.

The Alabama NAACP identified registered voters who had not cast a ballot in 2016 or who had been sporadic voters. With this list, local branches began calling, and calling, and calling. In addition, the NAACP set up phone banks so that volunteers in a number of other organizations, including Indivisible, a progressive grassroots network of local groups on a mission to "defeat the Trump agenda," could reach out to blacks in both urban and rural areas.

Based on research out of Stanford University, the activists knew that the message wasn't to ask whether someone was going to vote. Volunteers were instructed to use "'HIGH VOTER TURN-OUT' LANGUAGE AND ASK 'HIGH VOTER TURNOUT' QUESTIONS LIKE: 'I know you're a reliable/consistent voter' and 'We rely on reliable voters like you' and 'What time of day are you going to vote?'"

Staggering Facts
The NAACP, Indivisible, the Collective PAC, and BlackPAC . . .

- made 1.32 million phone calls

- mailed more than 220,000 postcards

- produced video ads that "garnered 1.4 million Facebook ad impressions, targeting 650,000 African American voters in every county in Alabama"

- sent one million texts

Face-to-face contact was crucial.

"We had a lot of Alabamians talking to Alabamians," remarked one member of Indivisible's Huntsville branch.

Randall Woodfin, the thirty-six-year-old mayor of Birmingham, who had previously won his own upset election victory, laid out the magic formula: "Doors. Doors. Doors. Turn ya folk out."

Woke Vote, a grassroots organization that was focused on the millennials, "centered its efforts on potential sites of latent black political power, including historically black colleges and universities and black churches," reported Newkirk. Woke Vote had "dozens of students working on 12 Alabama campuses" and had secured "11,000 signatures on a petition promising to cast a ballot," reported another journalist. Then the Sunday before the election, the organization deployed 270 canvassers, who "knocked on more than 14,000 doors . . . committing 6,000 voters on that day alone."

Meanwhile, with its eyes on black churches, Righteous Vote "had 120 captains representing 146 churches across Alabama," reported Will Drabold. Those congregations totaled more than 300,000 souls.

The NAACP's Mobile branch did the math and showed local ministers that they needed to take a fresh approach to turning out voters, which resulted in voter registration tables at church events and robo-calls targeting entire congregations.

All this outreach was impressive, but it all could have come to naught without the next component: seeing to it that people had access to the crucial information they needed to cast their ballots.

Alabama's voter ID law posed a formidable barrier. While the NAACP LDF, NAACP, and Greater Birmingham Ministries sued first to soften and then, hopefully, one day overturn the law, VoteRiders worked with grassroots organizations to launch voter ID clinics that helped folks get documents they needed for a voter ID.

Similarly, the NAACP set up call centers to deal with the confusion caused by the closure of sixty-six polling places. It also handled questions about what types of identification were acceptable and how to attain them, as well as queries, given Merrill's purge of more than three hundred thousand citizens from the voter rolls, about how to determine whether one was still registered to vote. In addition, at school alumni and reunion parties, NAACP branches also "handed out several thousand flyers with election dates, registration deadlines, absentee deadlines, [and] voter ID requirements." They followed up by distributing this same packet of vital information in their door-to-door canvassing. Still, the battle was far from won.

"Transportation to the polls is a HUGE issue in Alabama," is how Indivisible summed up yet another hurdle to voting for so many people.

To the rescue came Perman Hardy. Working solo, on Election Day, Hardy did what she has done for the past twenty-five years. She got into her vehicle and, over the course of the day, took to the polls fifty registered voters in Lowndes County who had no other way to get to the one voting machine at Old Bethel Baptist Church in Collirene. She convinced those who didn't think they were dressed well enough to step into a church and vote, she picked up sisters from their mobile home, and she shepherded a man from his job picking pecans to the polls and back to work in the orchard.

What Hardy did, multiplied across the state, was exactly what Alabama needed. And that's exactly what it got. Reminiscent of the highly effective private car service established during the 1956 Montgomery Bus Boycott, the NAACP and other organizations, such as Black Belt Citizens and Indivisible chapters in several counties, put in place a system of drivers, buses, and rideshares to get people to and from the polls.

None of this—the phone banks, the organizers going door-to-door, the vast information systems on the radio and social media and call centers, and getting voters to the polls—was cheap.

It cost money.

Senate Majority PAC, which was founded to counter the dark money pouring into the GOP, pumped over $6 million into Alabama. That funding helped finance the incredible ground game mounted by local organizations, including BlackPAC, which received $600,000—and which knocked on more than a half-million doors. "One key strategy that BlackPAC found especially useful," reported Newkirk, "was providing funds to pay organizers rather than relying on volunteers, a tactic that helped offset the strain and demands of canvassing rural and hard-to-reach communities in the state."

A week before the election, the Black Voters Matter Fund crowdfunded $200,000 to pay for more than four hundred canvassers in nineteen Alabama counties. In doing so, it provided, wrote Newkirk, "dozens of grants to smaller get-out-the-vote organizations, organized transportation to the polls, and printed thousands of pieces of voter literature."

This funding cyclone was augmented with resources from the NAACP, the Democratic National Committee, and Priorities USA, which focuses on traditional voter-mobilization techniques. Priorities USA, in fact, spent $1.5 million in Alabama, $1 million of which was "specifically spent on mobilizing black voters," reported *BuzzFeed News.*

All this effort, without question, was aided by the GOP's selecting one of the worst possible candidates imaginable. Roy Moore's well-documented litany of racist, sexist, homophobic, and anti–religious freedom stances should have made him immediately unacceptable. But it did not. Then . . .

On November 9, 2017, the *Washington Post* published a horrifying, well-researched story about Moore's serial attempts to date and sometimes sexually assault teenage girls while he was the assistant district attorney.

A few days later, the *New Yorker* published a piece on Moore's tendency to cruise the Gadsden mall looking for girls. The reporter, Charles Bethea, wrote that he "spoke or messaged with more than a dozen people—including a major political figure in the state—who told me that they had heard, over the years, that Moore had been banned from the mall because he repeatedly badgered teen-age girls." Revulsion began to course through some Republicans, but in the end many went back to supporting Moore.

Richard Shelby, the senior senator from Alabama, was among the Republicans who remained repulsed. A few days before the election, on CNN's Sunday show *State of the Union,* Shelby matter-of-factly remarked that when he cast his absentee ballot it was not for Roy Moore. "I think the Republican Party can do better," said Shelby. "The state of Alabama deserves better."

Shelby told viewers that on his absentee ballot he had written in the name of another Republican and urged others in Alabama to do likewise. His message was clear. Save the GOP and save Alabama by not voting for Moore.

The Democratic candidate had not been idle. Doug Jones rebuilt a disintegrated Democratic Party apparatus that had collapsed under the weight of the GOP's crushing victory in 2010. As the *New York Times* reported, Jones confronted a "Democratic operation [in Alabama] with the lights out. With a fairly anemic state party, there is little existing infrastructure for routine campaign activities like phone banks or canvassing drives." He put all of that in place.

Doug Jones also did serious outreach in the black community. He visited black churches many Sundays. He attended barbecues and fish frys. He spoke "about health care and jobs and infrastructure," said a Think Progress reporter. He reminded black people that he was the prosecutor who had successfully gone after the Klansmen who had planted the bomb in Birmingham's Sixteenth Street Baptist Church that killed those four little girls in 1963. Jones also advertised on billboards in black neighborhoods so that black voters knew his name, his credentials, and that he was not Roy Moore.

Yet when the much-anticipated Election Day rolled around on December 12, 2017, the hazards of being black and voting began to pop up almost immediately. Todd Cox, director of policy for the Legal Defense and Educational Fund, told TV host Roland Martin this: "We saw numerous examples of voter problems that confronted African Americans and their opportunity to participate in the electoral process. Voters standing in long lines only to be told they're on inactive lists and not being given the opportunity to vote on a regular ballot. Voters who, when they got there, were given false or incorrect information regarding the photo ID policies of Alabama. Voters who, unfortunately, in certain areas, stood in long lines because facilities lacked the proper or the right number of voter machines or check-in locations."

One news outlet reported that, according to Kristen Clarke, executive director of the Lawyers' Committee for Civil Rights Under Law, her organization "received about 300 calls from concerned voters before 4 p.m. A number of the calls were from voters—who had apparently not voted in a while—who'd been moved to 'inactive status.'"

Sherrilyn Ifill was also alerted to the problem of people on an inactive list along with a "shortage of ballots or wrong voting machines at certain African American precincts," as she later wrote in *Time* magazine. Too, there were "long lines in Selma and Mobile due to too-few voting machines or check-in tables."

Attorney and president and founder of the Transformative Justice Coalition, Barbara Arnwine, identified additional failings. Citizens "went into Montgomery to vote," she said, "and found out that the disability ramps had been removed." Given that 17.5 percent of adults in Montgomery County have disabilities, this was not inconsequential. Arnwine continued: "What we also saw was ex-felons who had had their rights restored attempting to vote and being denied that right because they would not accept their 'mugshot pictures' which had been agreed to be accepted as legitimate photo ID."

Organizations were ready for many of these shenanigans and

system failures. They had attorneys on the ground to assist with information about citizens' voting rights.

Meanwhile, Roy Moore had a lock on the Republican strongholds in most of the northern sectors of the state. As the vote tallies began to roll in, his lead continued to grow. But Moore's lead was not as large or as commanding as it should have been or would have been if he were a regular Republican candidate. The taint of Moore's behavior had clearly depressed the white voter turnout in Alabama. Too, Senator Shelby's call to moral arms was having an effect. There was a surge of write-in votes coming out of traditionally Republican counties as well. Indeed, nearly half the 22,819 write-ins came from counties that Moore carried. Moreover, college-educated whites, who had mostly backed Trump in 2016, were peeling off, too. For example, in Madison County, home to Huntsville, where both a major university and a NASA facility are located, the Republican presidential candidate had secured 54.85 percent of the vote. Yet in the 2017 special election, Moore eked out just a little over 46 percent. This was greater than an 8 percent drop and was an omen about what was to come. Meanwhile, Indivisible had focused its efforts on six counties. "Three of them—Madison, Lee, and Mobile—flipped from having a majority of their voters select Trump last November to a majority choosing Jones. In the other three counties . . . Houston, Dale, and Henry—the GOP's winning margins shrank by more than twenty points." But, even with all that, there was still a glimmer of hope on the Republican side.

Although the votes from the more diverse areas of the state had not yet been tallied, Moore still had a sizable lead. And if voter suppression worked as it was supposed to, and those in the

Black Belt counties and the cities stayed home, victory was assured, and, equally important, as in 2016, it would inevitably be chalked up to black people being disengaged and apathetic.

As the voted continued to be counted, black voters appeared to be up against the ropes—overwhelmed, outmatched, and headed for sure defeat at the hands of a much more powerful opponent. But then, a blazing uppercut caught Roy Moore squarely on the jaw and sent his hopes snapping back as "black people in Alabama punched above their weight," wrote Ryan C. Brooks with *BuzzFeed News*, and delivered an unexpected and well-delivered stunning blow. Fittingly, the first indication that Moore was in serious trouble came from a legendary place: Selma.

"Selma, Lord, Selma," tweeted Bernice King, daughter of Martin Luther King Jr., on election night. "It's no coincidence that Selma, where blood was shed in the struggle for voting rights for Black people, pushed #DougJones ahead for good."

As the election results kept rolling in, the black voter turnout surprised almost everyone.

If the overall voter turnout rate had been the paltry 25 percent that John Merrill had originally predicted, perhaps Moore, for whom Merrill reportedly cast his ballot, would have won. But "more than 40% of voters showed up, with surges well beyond 50% in counties favorable to Jones," reported Will Drabold with *Mic*. The people in the Black Belt counties, who were weighed down by everything that Alabama could throw at them, were equally impressive. As Drabold also reported: "[In Black Belt counties] which includes Dallas County, home of the city of

Selma, Jones won an average of 73.4% of the vote in counties with turnout that averaged 45.4%, about five percentage points higher than the state average, a *Mic* analysis found."

The Black Belt simply came through.

While Selma had Moore reeling, Birmingham truly delivered the knockout blow. There Jones picked up 83,213 more votes than Moore, Republican turnout was significantly less than in 2016, and there were 3,710 write-ins.

Roy Moore was down for the count.

There would be no getting up.

Roy Moore lost by 20,715 votes.

> "They never could see black people in Alabama, in a highly conservative racially polarized state . . . They never could see our power, even when we did."
> —LaTosha Brown, cofounder of the Black Voters Matter Fund and a native of Selma, on some media representations of a demoralized, low-energy, apathetic black community in a run-up to the special election

★ ★ ★ ★ ★

CONCLUSION

Propaganda posted to social media and linked to Russian interference during the 2016 election.

22

AT THE CROSSROADS

SOMETHING HAD GONE HORRIBLY WRONG. WHEN in February 2018, special counsel Robert Mueller indicted thirteen Russians for subverting the 2016 election, suspicions were confirmed. By weaponizing social media and exploiting the racial fissures in America, the Kremlin's agents had gone for the nation's Achilles' heel.

Pretending to be American citizens, Russian operatives opened up a series of social media accounts. After they earned their stripes as social justice warriors, they then began urging black people to boycott the election.

Using the Instagram account Woke Blacks, Russians posted a message suggesting that black people's disdain for Trump was simply manufactured by sinister influences trying to "forc[e] Blacks to vote Killary," with "Killary" being the pejorative social media name for Democratic presidential candidate Hillary

Clinton, who was cast as "the lesser of two devils." Faced with the distasteful choice between Trump, whom blacks were supposedly manipulated into loathing, and Clinton, that Instagram message stated, "we'd surely be better off without voting AT ALL."

On Facebook, Russians posted under the name Blacktivist, and eventually inflated their stature and profile using an internet bot farm that gave Blacktivist a larger following than that of Black Lives Matter.

Blacktivist then began posting about the upcoming 2016 election. "They would say things like: 'What have the Democrats done for you the last four years, the last 60 years'" recalled Katrina Martin-Boreau (a genuine black activist). "They would say: 'Show them your power by not showing up to vote.'" The message spread like a virulent toxin.

The Kremlin's agents didn't stop there. "They used the 'voter fraud' fantasy as well," explained Charles Pierce in *Esquire* magazine. Using the Twitter handle @TEN_GOP, in August 2016 Russians reported that an investigation was underway to uncover who had committed the latest round of voter fraud in North Carolina. Closer to Election Day, @TEN_GOP issued a tweet questioning the validity of tens of thousands of mail-in ballots for Hillary Clinton in Broward County, Florida, where more than half the population was Latino or black.

As insidious as all this was, the Russians, frankly, were merely piggybacking on the years of work done by the GOP to stigmatize, disenfranchise, and suppress the votes of black Americans and other people of color. As Reverend William Barber—another genuine black activist—so rightly put it: "Voter suppression hacked our democracy long before any Russian agents meddled in America's elections."

While there are far too many states that are eager to reduce "one person, one vote" to a meaningless phrase, others are determined to make "one person, one vote" 100 percent meaningful.

In 2015, Oregon pioneered in automatic voter registration (AVR). With AVR, unless they opt out, people eligible to vote are automatically registered to do so when they go to the DMV to get or renew driver's licenses. AVR went into effect January 2016. In four months, Oregon added 68,583 new voters to the rolls. By the end of July 2016, the number had risen to 222,197. What's more, its voter turnout rate in the 2016 election increased from 64 to 68 percent—"more than any other state," reported *The Nation* magazine. The income, age, and racial diversity of the electorate was enhanced by AVR, as was the participation of first-time and sporadic voters.

California's secretary of state Alex Padilla, dissatisfied with his own state's abysmal 42 percent voter turnout rate in 2014, had been scouring the nation for a way to boost it. California adopted, then adapted Oregon's AVR program to include preregistration of eligible sixteen- and seventeen-year-olds when they get a state ID or driver's license. These young women and men are automatically registered to vote when they turn eighteen.

Padilla had also installed observers, including himself, in Colorado during the November 2014 election. There they saw the effectiveness of same-day registration, which, studies show, can "boost turnout 7 to 14 percentage points," as a Think Progress post pointed out back in 2013.

These state initiatives to remove the barriers to the ballot box, including the use of mail-in ballots, which has had tremendous success in Colorado, are beginning to ricochet around the nation. As of 2019, sixteen states and the District of Columbia have implemented AVR.

Illinois and Rhode Island have expanded AVR to include other agencies beyond the DMV, such as social service agencies, that also have the capacity to electronically send verified files to election officials. That expansion to other major agencies is a big help to people who live in places with a great mass transit system and who cannot or choose not to drive and so have no reason to have contact with the DMV. It's worth noting that in Illinois the bill was bipartisan: Republicans and Democrats worked together to make voter registration easier. And the governor who signed the bill into law was a Republican.

Because the United States consistently ranks toward the bottom of developed democracies in terms of voter turnout, in June 2017, Democratic senators Patrick Leahy (Vermont), Dick Durbin (Illinois), and Amy Klobuchar (Minnesota) cosponsored legislation that would take AVR nationwide, but not one Republican in Congress has stepped up to support the bill: Automatic Voter Registration Act of 2017.

> "There is no reason why every eligible citizen cannot have the option of automatic registration when they visit the DMV, sign up for healthcare or sign up for classes in college."
> —Senator Patrick Leahy

In July 2017, Delaware eliminated the requirement for absentee ballots to be notarized, a boon to young men and women at a college or university out of state.

It was also in 2017 that New Mexico's state senate passed legislation to demolish the barrier that required citizens who wanted to cast a ballot to be registered to vote at least twenty-eight days before an election. The new bill knocked more than three weeks off that requirement and allows voting-eligible residents to register three days prior to an election.

Back in 2012, Connecticut passed legislation providing for same-day registration and online voter registration.

For years, Minnesota boasted the highest voter turnout rate in the nation, but the Democrats in the state senate were still not satisfied. In 2015, they passed a bill to extend early voting to "15 days before an election, expand mail-in balloting to small communities and permit convicted felons to vote immediately after they are released from prison." Republicans balked at the provisions, but it appears that their major resistance was "political. . . . In 2012, Barack Obama carried 17 of the 20 states that had the highest voter turnout."

In 2016, just to the east of Minnesota, Wisconsin's voter turnout dropped by more than sixty thousand. Two-thirds of that decline, by design, happened in Milwaukee. The Republican state leadership made it clear that it was willing to strangle into submission Democratic strongholds like the city that houses 70 percent of the state's black population. But now, the mayor and aldermen are fighting back. They have authorized funding to expand the number of early voting sites for Wisconsin's largest city from three in 2016 to eight in 2018. Similar efforts at expanding access to the franchise are occurring in Madison, Wisconsin; East Lansing, Michigan; New York City; St. Louis, Missouri; and Macon County, Illinois.

Yet, for all these efforts, there's still work to be done. The lie of rampant voter fraud has embedded itself into the American imagination and has proved resistant to facts, studies, court cases, and reports proving otherwise. As the tentacles of the lie continue to sink deeper and deeper into our democracy, they threaten to choke the very life out of the body politic and, in the end, severely weaken the United States.

Staggering Stats
In 2018, when it came to Americans eligible to vote . . .

- Seventy-seven million were not on the voter rolls. This number is more than the total combined population of the largest one hundred cities in America—from New York City to Birmingham—by nearly sixteen million people.

- Over 42 percent of Latino Americans were not registered to vote.

- Close to 43 percent of Asian Americans were not registered to vote.

- Almost 31 percent of black Americans were not registered.

- Only 26 percent of white Americans were not registered.

We're in trouble.

Years of gerrymandering, requiring IDs that only certain people have, illegally purging citizens from the voter rolls, and starving majority-people-of-color precincts of resources so as to create untenable conditions at the polls have exposed our electoral jugular and made the United States vulnerable to Russian attacks on our democracy. Those assaults played out as seamlessly as if they had been made in the USA and not hatched in the bowels of the Kremlin. But it's not just the Russian attack, as horrific as that is.

Voter suppression has made the US Senate wholly unrepresentative. Take Texas. In 2018, the Lone Star State had two Republican US senators, John Cornyn and Ted Cruz, who have voted overwhelmingly (97 percent and 92.5 percent, respectively) to support Trump's agenda regarding immigration, taxes, banking regulations that strip the requirement to report on discrimination in lending, and other policies. Yet, the senators' voting profile is antithetical to the composition of Texas, where "Latinos make up about 39% of the state's population."

Voter suppression has placed in the presidency a man who is anything but presidential. It has already reshaped the US Supreme Court with the installation of Neil Gorsuch and Brett Kavanaugh, threatening to undermine the judiciary for decades to come.

Thus, when thirty-one states are vying to develop new and more ruthless ways to disenfranchise their populations, and when others are searching desperately for ways to bring millions of citizens into the electorate, we have created a nation where democracy is simultaneously atrophying and growing—depending solely on where one lives.

History makes clear, however, that this is simply not sustainable.

It wasn't sustainable in the antebellum era.

It wasn't sustainable when the poll tax and literacy test gave disproportionate power in Congress to Southern Democrats. And it's certainly not sustainable now.

> "When more citizens participate in our democracy, our democracy is stronger."
>
> —State Senator Jeff Steinborn of New Mexico
>
> "We know that when voters are given the opportunity to vote, that voters vote."
>
> —Scot Ross, former executive director of One Wisconsin Now and One Wisconsin Institute

DISCUSSION GUIDE

1. This book's title is a modification of the saying "one person, one vote." What do you think this variation means?

2. Voting is often declared to be the cornerstone of democracy. Why do you think that is?

3. The current age to vote in the United States is eighteen. Do you think this is the right age? Why or why not?

4. Combating voter suppression is essential to maintaining fair elections. Why, then, don't all candidates for political office speak out on the topic?

5. What are some ways in which voter suppression is tied to America's legacy of slavery?

6. Why do you think the myth of voter fraud has maintained its popularity?

7. In 1920, the Nineteenth Amendment was ratified, granting women the right to vote. How do you think race factored into the implementation of this amendment?

8. Whose responsibility is it to fight voter suppression? How should they do so?

9. Some technological advances, like Exact Match and sophisticated mapping software, have resulted in increased voter suppression. What are ways that technology can combat suppression?

10. What's your criteria for a fair election?

GET INVOLVED IN YOUR COMMUNITY

There are lots of ways to get involved with voting in your own community. Here are a few.

REGISTER

If you're eighteen and a documented citizen who, in most states, is not in prison or on parole for a felony, you have the right to vote. In many states, you need to register ahead of time. Every state has different rules, so check with your local election office—you can locate your office at https://www.usa.gov/register-to-vote. Don't forget to allow plenty of time before the election you'd like to participate in—many states require registration at least several weeks in advance.

HELP OTHER VOTERS

If you're too young or can't register yourself, you can still help others! Use those same local election websites to help family, friends, and neighbors register, confirm registrations are up-to-date, check information on absentee and early voting rules, and locate polling places. Make sure people have a voting plan—that is, ask others how and when they will go to vote.

RESEARCH

Find out what exactly will appear on your ballot—you might be voting for more candidates and topics than you expected. Most states will provide sample ballots on their websites. Many individual groups, including nonprofits, will put together resources that list recommendations of who to vote for. These can be valuable resources, but always check for the fine print that tells you the name of the group making the suggestions—that way, you can decide if their interests align with yours. The best research is always your own, so read, watch, and listen all you can.

VOLUNTEER

If there's a candidate you love, give your time. Phone banking can make a big difference. If you're interested in an election, but it's not taking place where you live, you might still be able to call on behalf of the candidates. Check the candidate's website for information.

NOTES

PROLOGUE

p. xi: "simply saw no affirmative reason": Jesse Singal, "Why Black Voters in Milwaukee Weren't Enthused by Hillary Clinton," *New York Magazine*, November 22, 2016, nymag.com/daily/intelligencer/2016/11/why-black-voters-in-milwaukee-werent-enthused-by-clinton.html, accessed March 11, 2017.

p. xi: "African-American, Latino and younger voters failed to show up at the polls in sufficient numbers": Tami Luhby, "How Hillary Clinton Lost," CNN, November 9, 2016, www.cnn.com/2016/11/09/politics/clinton-votes-african-americans-latinos-women-white-voters, accessed March 11, 2017.

p. xii: on the drop in voter turnout among black, Latino, and Asian Americans: Reid Wilson, "Voter Turnout Dipped in 2016, Led by Decline Among Blacks," *The Hill*, May 11, 2017, thehill.com/homenews/campaign/332970-voter-turnout-dipped-in-2016-led-by-decline-among-blacks, accessed June 29, 2017.

PART ONE: A HISTORY OF DISENFRANCHISEMENT

1. BUBBLES IN A BAR OF SOAP

p. 3: "of the people, by the people, and for the people":
"Gettysburg Address," Abraham Lincoln, November 19, 1863.

p. 4: "the laws relative to finance": Thomas E. Miller quoted
in John Hope Franklin and Alfred A. Moss Jr., *From Slavery to
Freedom: A History of African Americans*, 8th ed. (Boston: McGraw Hill,
2000), 287.

p. 4: "No negro is fit": A. A. Taylor, "Democracy Crushed by Caste,"
Journal of Negro History 11, no. 3 (July 1926): 519.

p. 4: "Many Texans refused to accept": Maude Cuney Hare
quoted in Henry Allen Bullock, "The Expansion of Negro Suffrage in
Texas," *Journal of Negro Education* 26, no. 3 (Summer 1957): 370.

**p. 5: "eliminate the darkey" and Glass's exchange with fellow
delegate:** Michael Waldman, *The Fight to Vote* (New York: Simon and
Schuster, 2016), 85.

**p. 5: "the ignorant and vicious white . . . this great
franchise":** Waldman, *The Fight to Vote*, 84.

p. 6: Bilbo's remarks: US Commission on Civil Rights, "Voting in
Mississippi," 5, www.law.umaryland.edu/marshall/usccr/documents
/crl2v94.pdf, accessed July 12, 2017.

**p. 6: on the educational attainment of black adults in
1940 in Mississippi, South Carolina, Louisiana, Georgia,
and Alabama:** Jessie Parkhurst Guzman, ed., *Negro Year Book: A Review of
Events Affecting Negro Life, 1941–1946* (Tuskegee, AL: Tuskegee Institute,
1947), 70.

**p. 6: on spending on black and white elementary
schoolchildren in Louisiana:** Carol Anderson, *White Rage: The
Unspoken Truth of Our Racial Divide* (New York: Bloomsbury, 2017,
paperback ed.), 70.

p. 7: Leon Alexander's ordeal: William H. Chafe, Raymond
Gavins, and Robert Korstad, *Remembering Jim Crow: African Americans
Tell About Life in the Segregated South* (New York: New Press, 2001),
277–80.

p. 8: "bubbles?": David C. Colby, "The Voting Rights Act and Black Registration in Mississippi," *Publius* 16, no. 4 (Autumn 1986): 127.

2. POLL TAX BLUES

p. 11: "the revival of the poll tax. . . . pay the tax for him": "Disenfranchisement by Means of the Poll Tax," *Harvard Law Review* 53, no. 4 (1940): 647fn15.

p. 12: "less than $100 a year": G. C. Stoney, "Suffrage in the South—Part I: The Poll Tax," Social Welfare History Project, Virginia Commonwealth University, January 1, 1940, socialwelfare.library.vcu.edu /issues/suffrage-south-poll-tax/, accessed July 6, 2017.

pp. 12–13: "paying a poll tax in February": Stoney, "Suffrage in the South—Part I: The Poll Tax."

p. 13: "instructed his deputies . . . registered to vote": US Civil Rights Commission, "Voting in Mississippi," 19.

p. 13: "receipts are not only bought" and "buy up as many poll tax receipts": Stoney, "Suffrage in the South—Part I: The Poll Tax."

pp. 13–14: on turnout in seven poll states in midterm elections and turnout in 1944 presidential election: Berg, *The Ticket to Freedom*, 105; David M. Jordan, *FDR, Dewey, and the Election of 1944* (Bloomington: Indiana University Press, 2011), 322.

3. ONLY DEMOCRATS NEED APPLY

p. 18: "emasculate politically the entire body of Negro voters": Leo Alilunas, "The Rise of the 'White Primary' Movement as a Means of Barring the Negro from the Polls," *Journal of Negro History* 25, no. 2 (April 1940): 162.

p. 18: "a more brutally direct fashion . . . the Fourteenth Amendment": Thurgood Marshall, "The Rise and Collapse of the 'White Democratic Primary,'" *Journal of Negro Education* 26, no. 3 (Summer 1957): 251.

p. 19: "immune from the strictures of the Fourteenth and Fifteenth Amendments": *United States v. Cruikshank*, 92 US 542 (1875).

pp. 19, 20: "could be excluded . . . pierced the façade": Marshall, "The Rise and Collapse," 251–52.

p. 20: "If a state law made . . ." and "One thing is certain": Darlene Clark Hine, "Blacks and the Destruction of the Democratic White Primary, 1935–1944," *Journal of Negro History* 62, no. 1 (January 1977): 44.

p. 20: "looked behind the law": Marshall, "The Rise and Collapse," 253.

4. AND DON'T FORGET THE MATCHES

pp. 23, 24: on the rise in registered black voters in Georgia, Talmadage's tactics and "The first Negro to vote will never vote again": Patricia Sullivan, *Lift Every Voice: The NAACP and the Making of the Civil Rights Movement* (New York: New Press, 2009), 318–19.

p. 25: "red-blooded Anglo-Saxon . . . the matches": Carol Anderson, *Eyes Off the Prize: The United Nations and the African American Struggle for Human Rights, 1944–1955* (New York: Cambridge University Press, 2003), 63–64.

5. HERE COMES THE VRA

p. 30: "numerous examples of racial terrorism . . . the brutal persecution": "Who Is Violating the Rights of Man?," *Current Digest of the Russian Press* 8, no. 50 (January 23, 1957): 23.

p. 31: "National guard soldiers and policemen": "This Must Be Said!," *Current Digest of the Russian Press* 9, no. 37 (October 23, 1957): 25.

p. 31: "see clearly the harm": Jason C. Parker, *Hearts, Minds, and Voices: US Cold War Public Diplomacy and the Formation of the Third World* (New York: Oxford University Press, 2016), 109.

p. 31: "Armed Men Cordon Off": Mary L. Dudziak, *Cold War Civil Rights: Race and the Image of American Democracy* (Princeton, NJ: Princeton University Press, 2000), 119.

p. 33: on how long and drawn out suits were: Allan Lichtman, "The Federal Assault Against Voting Discrimination in the Deep South, 1957–1967," *Journal of Negro History* 54, no. 4 (October 1969): 364.

p. 35: "thrust the federal government": Waldman, *The Fight to Vote*, 149.

p. 35: "can complete something": Extension of the 1965 Voting Rights Act: Greensboro-Selma Hearings, Box 228, Folder 19, Papers of the Southern Christian Leadership Conference, Stuart Rose Library, Woodruff Library, Emory University, Atlanta, Georgia.

6. THE WAR ON THE VRA

p. 40: "The Voting Rights Act was designed ": *South Carolina v. Katzenbach* (1966).

p. 41: "preserve our way of doing business": Gary May, *Bending Toward Justice: The Voting Rights Act and the Transformation of American Democracy* (Durham, NC, and London: Duke University Press, 2015), 209.

p. 42: "all action necessary to make a vote effective . . . because of race": *Allen v. State Board of Elections* (1969).

p. 42: "so distorts our constitutional structure": *South Carolina v. Katzenbach* (1966).

p. 42: on the rise in black voter registration: Alexander Keyssar, *The Right to Vote: The Contested History of Democracy in the United States* (New York: Basic Books, 2000), 212.

p. 44: "confusing," "conflicting" . . . "hodgepodge": Reginald Stuart, "2 Alabama Rights Workers Are Jailed for Voting Fraud," *New York Times*, January 12, 1982.

p. 45: on the Spanns' coziness with members of law enforcement and "The sentences are believed": Art Harris, "Pickens County Flare-Up: The Story of 2 Blacks Found Guilty," *Washington Post*, February 6, 1982, washingtonpost.com/archive/politics /1982/02/06/pickens-county-flare-up-the-story-of-2-blacks-found-guilty /5fdc01a5-35f2-46a7-94eb-01bba7e47418/?noredirect=on&utm_term= .b1608e5f2d66, accessed March 20, 2019.

p. 45: "to get to the polls" "for trying to make democracy work," and "We have a policy . . . because they are black": Harris, "Pickens County Flare-Up."

p. 46: "The women spent . . . release assignment": UPI, November 10, 1982, https://www.upi.com/Archives/1982/11/10/Two

-black-women-whose-voting-fraud-convictions-triggered-a/6761405752400/, accessed March 20, 2019.

p. 48: "credible" "degrading . . . to say" "first and last" "done with voting": Emily Bazelon, "The Voter Fraud Case Jeff Sessions Lost and Can't Escape," *New York Times Magazine*, January 9, 2017.

p. 48: "Ninety-two-year-old Willie Bright": Ari Berman, "Jeff Sessions, Trump's Pick for Attorney General, Is a Fierce Opponent of Civil Rights," *The Nation*, November 18, 2016, https://www.thenation.com /article/jeff-sessions-trumps-pick-for-attorney-general-is-a-fierce-opponent -of-civil-rights/, accessed June 10, 2019.

p. 49: "the criminal processes": Sanders and Beal, "Defending Voting Rights in the Alabama Black Belt," *The Black Scholar*, May/June 1986, 26, 34.

p. 49: "I'll never forget": Scott Zamost, Drew Griffin, and Curt Devine, "Woman Prosecuted by Jeff Sessions Can't Forgive," CNN, January 9, 2017, accessed July 27, 2017.

7. A "JUDICIAL COUP D'ÉTAT"

p. 52: on the shrinking of Bush's margin of victory: David Margolick, "The Path to Florida," *Vanity Fair*, March 19, 2014, www.vanity fair.com/news/2004/10/florida-election-2000, accessed July 22, 2017.

p. 53: "judicial coup d'état": Vincent Bugliosi, *The Betrayal of America: How the Supreme Court Undermined the Constitution and Chose Our President* (New York: Thunder's Mouth Press/Nation Books, 2001), 42.

p. 54: "the same states and counties": Keyssar, *The Right to Vote*, 214.

p. 55: "racial discrimination was no longer": Keyssar, *The Right to Vote*, 215.

p. 55: on Rehnquist's anti–voting rights activities: Anderson, *White Rage*, 143.

p. 56: "The enforcement provisions of the Civil War Amendments"; "Rehnquist reinforced . . . Rehnquist philosophy"; "I remember him being a zealot"; "In the seven southern . . . none to some": Ari Berman, "Inside John Roberts' Decades-Long Crusade Against the Voting Rights Act," *Politico*,

August 10, 2015, www.politico.com/magazine/story/2015/08/john
-roberts-voting-rights-act-121222, accessed July 23, 2017.

PART TWO: VOTER ID

8. "A CITIZEN NO MORE"

p. 65: "I wasn't a citizen no more": Omar Villafranca, "Texas'
Voter ID Law Is 'Unexplainable on Grounds Other Than Race,' Federal
Judge Rules," CBS News, April 13, 2017, www.cbsnews.com/news/army
-vet-86-leads-suit-against-texas-voter-id-law/, accessed May 19, 2017.

p. 66: "bureaucratic nightmare" and "The intent of this law":
Sari Horwitz, "Getting a Photo ID So You Can Vote Is Easy. Unless
You're Poor, Black, Latino, or Elderly," *Washington Post*, May 23, 2016,
www.washingtonpost.com/politics/courts_law/getting-a-photo-id-so-you
-can-vote-is-easy-unless-youre-poor-black-latino-or-elderly/2016/05/23
/8d5474ec-20f0-11e6-8690-f14ca9de2972_story.html, accessed
September 9, 2017.

p. 66: Letter to Governor Abbott: Jeremiah "Jay" Prophet,
"An Open Letter from One Disabled Person to Another," *Texas Tribune*,
July 21, 2017, https://www.tribtalk.org/2017/07/21/an-open-letter-from
-one-disabled-person-to-another/ accessed July 22, 2017.

p. 67: "Coming home . . . very frustrating": Christina A. Cassidy,
"In Wisconsin, ID Law Proved Insurmountable for Many Voters," AP
News, May 14, 2017, apnews.com/dafac088c90242ef8b282fbebddf5b56,
accessed May 14, 2017.

9. FLORIDA FIASCO, MISSOURI MADNESS, HOOSIER STATE HORRORS, AND GEORGIA NOT SO PEACHY KEEN

**p. 69: "put great stress on the public's faith in electoral
integrity" and "a wake-up call":** Richard L. Hasen, *The Voting Wars:
From Florida 2000 to the Next Election Meltdown* (New Haven, CT: Yale
University Press, 2012), 5.

**pp. 70–71: "chaotic mess;" "By early evening;" and "represents
the biggest fraud":** Lorraine C. Minnite, *The Myth of Voter Fraud*
(Ithaca, NY, and London: Cornell University Press, 2010), 99–101.

p. 71: "conspiracy to create": Hasen, *The Voting Wars*, 47.

pp. 72–73: "provocative . . . sowed confusion": Margolick, "The Path to Florida."

pp. 74–75: "wrongly classified . . . residences"; "snared"; "more than eight people"; "suspect voters"; and "none of these problems": Brennan Center for Justice, "Missouri, 2000," https://www.brennancenter.org/analysis/missouri-2000, accessed March 20, 2019.

p. 76: "as many as 19 million . . . African American": Keyssar, *The Right to Vote*, 284.

p. 76: "protect the integrity of the ballot box" and "civic-minded": Zachary Roth, *The Great Suppression: Voting Rights, Corporate Cash* (New York: Crown, 2016), 23.

p. 77: "the only prominent nongovernmental . . . harder for people to vote": Hasen, "The Fraudulent Fraud Squad: The Incredible, Disappearing American Center for Voting Rights," *Slate*, May 18, 2007, www.slate.com/articles/news_and_politics/jurisprudence/2007/05/the_fraudulent_fraud_squad.html, accessed September 24, 2017.

p. 78: ACVR claim of NAACP paying for votes with crack cocaine: "Stranger Than Fiction: Nexis Search Shows the Media's Reported Nexus Between ACORN and Crack Cocaine (Hey, Don't Blame Us: We're Just the Messengers.)," Capital Research Center, October 31, 2008, capitalresearch.org/article/stranger-than-fiction-nexis-search-shows-the-medias-reported-nexus-between-acorn-and-crack-cocaine-hey-dont-blame-us-were-just-the-messengers/, accessed October 1, 2017.

p. 78: "In 2005": Hasen, *The Voting Wars*, 51.

p. 79: on the thirteen-year-old boy: Alex Koppelman, "How U.S. Attorneys Were Used to Spread Voter-Fraud Fears," *Salon*, March 21, 2007, www.salon.com/2007/03/21/us_attorneys_2/, accessed September 24, 2017.

p. 79: "There was nothing that we uncovered": Eric Lipton and Ian Urbina, "In 5-Year Effort, Scant Evidence of Voter Fraud," *New York Times*, April 12, 2007, www.nytimes.com/2007/04/12/washington/12fraud.html, accessed September 24, 2017.

pp. 81–82: "Byzantine requirements"; "Catch-22"; "made multiple fruitless"; and "constitutional danger sign": *Crawford v. Marion County Election Board et al.*, Reply Brief for Petitioners, No. 07-21, /publishing/preview/publiced_preview_briefs_pdfs_07_08_07_21 _PetitionerReply.authcheckdam.pdf, accessed September 29, 2017.

p. 82: "Any valid state": "Voter ID," Georgia Department of Driver Services, accessed February 22, 2019.

p. 84: "did not conduct"; Burmeister statements: "Black Lawmakers: Burmeister Should Resign Her Position," *Athens Banner-Herald*, November 24, 2005, onlineathens.com/stories/112405 /news_20051124053.shtml#.WdBQA7pFw5t, accessed September 30, 2017.

p. 85: "on the ground that the state": Section 5 Recommendation Memorandum: Factual Investigation and Legal Review, August 25, 2005, Brennan Center for Justice, /sites/default/files/analysis/08 -25-05%20 Georgia%20ID%20Preclearance%20Memo%20 -%20DOJ%20Staff.pdf, accessed September 30, 2017.

p. 85: "strictest": Suevon Lee and Sarah Smith, "Everything You've Ever Wanted to Know About Voter ID Laws," ProPublica, March 9, 2016, www.propublica.org/article/everything-youve-ever -wanted-to-know-about-voter-id-laws, accessed March 12, 2017.

10. FLOODGATES OPENED WIDE

p. 88: "before the midterm elections": Dan Balz, "The GOP Takeover in the States," *Washington Post*, November 13, 2010, www .washingtonpost.com/wp-dyn/content/article/2010/11/13 /AR2010111302389.html, accessed October 1, 2017.

p. 88: "180 bills to restrict . . . the franchise": Nancy MacLean, *Democracy in Chains: The Deep History of the Radical Right's Stealth Plan for America* (New York: Viking, 2017), xvi.

p. 88: "everybody to vote": Ari Berman, *Give Us the Ballot: The Modern Struggle for Voting Rights in America* (New York: Farrar, Straus and Giroux, 2015), 260.

p. 89: "a time in American history": Zachary Roth, *The Great Suppression*, 24.

p. 89: "between 1982 and 2006 . . . the political process":
Justice Ginsburg dissent, *Shelby County v. Holder.*

p. 90: "nearly half of Americans": Michael Wines, "How Charges of Voter Fraud Became a Political Strategy," *New York Times*, October 21, 2016, /2016/10/22/us/how-charges-of-voter-fraud-became-a-political-strategy.html, accessed May 16, 2017.

p. 90: "a handful of GOP Senators": Michael Wines, "Some Republicans Acknowledge Leveraging Voter ID Laws for Political Gain," *New York Times*, September 16, 2016, www.nytimes.com/2016/09/17/us/some-republicans-acknowledge-leveraging-voter-id-laws-for-political-gain.html, accessed May 16, 2017.

pp. 90–91: emails about Judge David Prosser's race: Charles P. Pierce, "People Have a Right to Vote. Period. More evidence that Voter ID laws are about voter suppression," *Esquire*, September 15, 2016, /a48625/wisconsin-voter-suppression-republicans/, accessed April 15, 2018.

p. 91: on non-voter fraud in North Carolina: "Now We Finally Know How Bad Voter Fraud Is in North Carolina," editorial, *Charlotte Observer*, April 24, 2017, www.charlotteobserver.com/opinion/editorials/article146486019.html, accessed April 25, 2017.

p. 93: on NAACP LDF study: Kent Faulk, "NAACP Legal Defense Fund: More Than 100,000 Alabama Registered Voters Can't Cast a Ballot," AL.com, March 4, 2017, /03/naacp_legal_defense_fund_more.html, accessed March 5, 2017.

p. 93: "worst voter suppression law": Ian Millhiser, "Breaking: America's Worst Voter Suppression Law Won't Take Effect for This Election," ThinkProgress, August 31, 2016, thinkprogress.org/breaking-americas-worst-voter-suppression-law-won-t-take-effect-for-this-election-773aaa719f20, accessed July 21, 2017.

p. 93: "rate than white registered": Brynna Quillin, "Why Current Voter ID Laws Are Harmful to American Democracy," *Kennedy School Review*, May 28, 2017, harvardkennedyschoolreview.com/why-current-voter-id-laws-are-harmful-to-american-democracy/, accessed June 11, 2017.

p. 94: "with almost surgical precision . . . conceal the state's true motivation": Robert Barnes, "Supreme Court Won't Review

Decision That Found N.C. Voting Law Discriminates Against African
Americans," *Washington Post*, May 15, 2017, https://www.washingtonpost
.com/politics/courts_law/supreme-court-wont-review-decision-that-found
-nc-voting-law-discriminates-against-african-americans/2017/05/15
/59425b1c-2368-11e7-a1b3-faff0034e2de_story.html?utm_term=.00622e
046979, accessed March 20, 2019.

p. 94: "which white people": "A Judge Ruled Texas's Second Try at
Voter ID Laws Is Illegal. She's Right," editorial, *Washington Post*,
August 26, 2017, www.washingtonpost.com/opinions/a-judge-ruled
-texass-second-try-at-voter-id-laws-is-illegal-shes-right/2017/08/26
/4c565476-891b-11e7-961d-2f373b3977ee_story.html, accessed
August 28, 2017.

p. 94: "brushed aside geographical": Lee and Smith, "Everything
You've Ever Wanted to Know About Voter ID Laws."

p. 95: "exceptionally narrow": NAACP LDF, "Texas Court Order
Helps Combat Misinformation Given to Voters," September 19, 2016,
accessed October 1, 2017.

p. 95: "the turnout gaps . . . deterred": Mirren Gidda, "Why It Is
So Hard to Vote If You're Black, Poor or Elderly in America," *Newsweek*,
April 11, 2017, www.newsweek.com/voter-id-laws-texas-minority-voters
-strict-states-582405, accessed May 20, 2017.

p. 95: "suggests that voter ID laws": Sarah Childress, "Why Voter
ID Laws Aren't Really About Fraud," *Frontline*, October 20, 2014,
accessed April 26, 2017.

p. 96: "at the mercy" and "wretched failure": Todd Richmond,
"Judge Rips Wisconsin Officials Over Voter ID Law Confusion," *Seattle
Times*, October 12, 2016, www.seattletimes.com/nation-world/judge
-criticizes-wisconsin-for-confusing-info-on-voting-id/, accessed October 1,
2017.

PART THREE: VOTER ROLL PURGE

11. AND KEMP SAW DEAD PEOPLE

p. 101: Virginia voter roll purge: Greg Palast, "The GOP's Stealth
War Against Voters," *Rolling Stone*, August 24, 2016, /the-gops-stealth-war
-against-voters-w435890, accessed May 17, 2017.

p. 101: Indiana voter purge: Max Greenwood, "Indiana Purges Nearly 500,000 from Voter Rolls," *The Hill*, April 20, 2017, thehill.com /blogs/ballot-box/329659-indiana-purges-nearly-half-a-million-from -voter-rolls, accessed May 16, 2017.

p. 101: Georgia voter purge: Kristina Torres, "Georgia Cancels Registration of More Than 591,500 Voters," *Atlanta Journal-Constitution*, July 31, 2017, www.myajc.com/news/state—regional-govt—politics /georgia-cancels-registration-more-than-591-500-voters /ozSuX227UpNe18YGQ0hYUJ/, accessed November 26, 2017.

p. 101: Ohio voter purge: Ari Berman, "Trump Administration on the Right to Vote: Use It or Lose It," *Mother Jones*, August 8, 2017, /politics/2017/08/trump-administration-on-the-right-to-vote-use-it-or -lose-it/, accessed August 11, 2017.

pp. 101–02: on low voter turnout and "When there's no organizing": Richard L. Berke, "Experts Say Low 1988 Turnout May Be Repeated," *New York Times*, November 13, 1988, www.nytimes.com /1988/11/13/us/experts-say-low-1988-turnout-may-be-repeated.html, accessed December 5, 2017.

p. 102: on difficulty registering in Mississippi and Indianapolis and "from 1972 to 1992": J. Mijin Cha, "Registering Millions: Celebrating the Success and Potential of the National Voter Registration Act at 20," *Demos*, /registering-millions -success-and-potential-national-voter-registration-act-20, accessed November 27, 2017.

pp. 102–03: "is a fundamental right . . . including racial minorities": National Voter Registration Act of 1993, Pub. L. 103-31, 107 Stat. 77 (1993). www.gpo.gov/fdsys/pkg/STATUTE-107/pdf /STATUTE-107-Pg77.pdf, accessed March 28, 2018.

p. 103: on the increase in registered voters: Federal Election Commission, "The Impact of the National Voter Registration Act of 1993 on the Administration of Elections for Federal Office 1995–1996," www .eac.gov/assets/1/6/The%20Impact%20of%20the%20National%20 Voter%20Registration%20Act%20on%20Federal%20Elections%201995 -1996.pdf, accessed November 27, 2017.

pp. 103–04: on voter roll guidelines: National Voter Registration Act of 1993, 103rd Congress, 1st sess.

p. 105: on Ohio's 2011–2016 purge: Berman, "Trump Administration on the Right to Vote: Use It or Lose It."

p. 105: "felt embarrassed and stupid": Ari Berman, "The Supreme Court Could Make It Easier for States to Purge Voters," *The Nation*, May 30, 2017, /article/supreme-court-make-easier-states-purge -voters/, accessed May 30, 2017.

p. 106: "I'm a veteran": Hannah Yi, Mori Rothman, and Chris Bury, "Why Ohio Has Purged at Least 200,000 from the Voter Rolls," *PBS NewsHour*, July 31, 2016, /newshour/bb/inside-ohios-fight-voting-rules/, accessed May 17, 2017.

p. 106: "updated its elections law to . . . otherwise eligible": Leigh Chapman, "Ohio: Protect the Voter Rolls from Illegal Purges That Make It Harder for Eligible Citizens to Vote," Let America Vote, August 30, 2017, policy.letamericavote.org/case-study-ohio-voter-purge -161aa76f43dc, accessed October 10, 2017.

pp. 106–07: "If this is really [an] important . . . done so within a six-year period": David A. Graham, "Ohio's Questionable Voter Purge," *Atlantic*, June 3, 2016, accessed October 7, 2017.

p. 107: "white voters are 21 percent more likely": Palast, "The GOP's Stealth War Against Voters."

pp. 107–08: "voters in neighborhoods . . . less than 40 percent of the vote": Ari Berman, "As the GOP Convention Begins, Ohio Is Purging Tens of Thousands of Democratic Voters," *The Nation*, July 18, 2016, https://www.thenation.com/article/as-the-gop-convention-begins-ohio-is -purging-tens-of-thousands-of-democratic-voters/, accessed July 19, 2016.

p. 108: "white rural areas went nearly untouched": Anderson, *White Rage*, 163.

pp. 108–09: "investigated voter-registration drives . . . no charges were filed": Michael Wines, "Critics See Efforts by Counties and Towns to Purge Minority Voters from Rolls," *New York Times*, July 31, 2016, www.nytimes.com/2016/08/01/us/critics-see-efforts-to-purge-mino rities-from-voter-rolls-in-new-elections-rules.html, accessed May 17, 2017.

p. 109: "registration status canceled 'due to failure to vote'": Torres, "Suit Alleges That Georgia Is Illegally Bumping Voters off Rolls,"

The Atlanta Journal-Constitution, February 11, 2016, accessed March 20, 2019.

p. 109: "secretary of state's office does not 'purge' any voters":
Tony Pugh, "Georgia Secretary of State Fighting Accusations of Disenfranchising Minority Voters," McClatchyDC, October 7, 2016, www.mcclatchydc.com/news/politics-government/article106692837.html, accessed November 26, 2017.

p. 109: "voter list maintenance": Torres, "Georgia Cancels Registration of More than 591,500 Voters," *The Atlanta Journal-Constitution*, July 31, 2017, https://www.ajc.com/news/state—regional -govt—politics/georgia-cancels-registration-more-than-591-500-voters /ozSuX227UpNe18YGQ0hYUJ/, accessed March 20, 2019.

p. 109–10: "examining approximately 2.1 million":
Christopher Ingraham, "7 Papers, 4 Government Inquiries, 2 News Investigations and 1 Court Ruling Proving Voter Fraud Is Mostly a Myth," *Washington Post*, July 9, 2014, /news/wonk/wp/2014/07/09/7 -papers-4-government-inquiries-2-news-investigations-and-1-court-ruling -proving-voter-fraud-is-mostly-a-myth/, accessed December 7, 2017.

12. EXACT MATCH AND CROSSCHECK

p. 114: "Of nearly 35,000 registration forms . . . applications halted": Pugh, "Georgia Secretary of State Fighting Accusations of Disenfranchising Minority Voters."

p. 115: "has been a key architect": Tomas Lopez and Jennifer L. Clark, "Uncovering Kris Kobach's Anti-Voting History," Brennan Center for Justice, May 11, 2017, /blog/uncovering-kris-kobach%E2%80%99s -anti-voting-history, accessed May 27, 2017.

p. 115: "My hope is that Kansas": Ari Berman, "The Man Behind Trump's Voter Fraud Obsession: How Kris Kobach, the Kansas Secretary of State, Plans to Remake America Through Restrictive Voting and Immigration Laws," *New York Times*, June 13, 2017, /magazine /the-man-behind-trumps-voter-fraud-obsession.html, accessed June 13, 2017.

pp. 115–16: on the Brewers: Mark Joseph Stern, "The Presidential Advisory Commission on Election Mendacity: The First Public Meeting

of Trump's Voter Fraud Panel Was a Horrifying Parade of Outright
Lies," *Slate*, July 19, 2017, prudence/2017/07/the_first_public_meeting
_of_trump_s_voter_fraud_panel_was_a_parade_of_lies.html, accessed
July 19, 2017.

p. 116: "Kobach uses every": Roxana Hegeman, "Uncounted Ballots
Fuel Fears About Kobach's Proposals," KIRO 7 News, August 23, 2017,
www.kiro7.com/news/uncounted-kansas-ballots-fuel-fears-about-kobachs
-proposals/596788663, accessed August 23, 2017.

p. 116: "1) present photo IDs prior": Chelsie Bright, "Kris Kobach
and Kansas' SAFE Act," The Conversation, July 26, 2017,
theconversation.com/kris-kobach-and-kansas-safe-act-81314, accessed
December 8, 2017.

p. 116: "com[e] here to vote": Vann R. Newkirk II, "What's the Real
Goal of Trump's Voter-Fraud Commission?," *Atlantic*, July 26, 2017,
/politics/archive/2017/07/trump-vote-fraud-commission/534843/,
accessed July 26, 2017.

p. 117: "We had margins": Ben Strauss, " 'Kris Kobach Came After
Me for an Honest Mistake,' " *Politico*, May 21, 2017, www.politico.com
/magazine/story/2017/05/21/kris-kobach-voter-fraud-investigation
-prosecution-215164, accessed May 22, 2017.

p. 117: "the tip of the iceberg": Ben Strauss, " 'Kris Kobach Came
After Me for an Honest Mistake,' " *Politico*, May 21, 2017, /05/21
/kris-kobach-voter-fraud-investigation-prosecution-215164, accessed
May 22, 2017.

**p. 117: "associated minority voters with 'ethnic cleansing' . . .
with illegal aliens":** Sherrilyn Ifill, "President Trump's Election
Integrity Commission Is Illegal and Unconstitutional—That's Why We
Filed a Lawsuit," *Salon*, July 27, 2017, www.salon.com/2017/07/27
/president-trumps-election-integrity-commission-is-illegal-and
-unconstitutional-that-is-why-we-filed-a-lawsuit/, accessed July 27, 2017.

**p. 117: "may disparately impact voters . . . an
unconstitutional poll tax" and "is not worth the paper that it
was written on":** Jim McLean, "Report: Kansas Election Law
Suppressing Turnout," KCUR, March 14, 2017, kcur.org/post-report
-kansas-election-law-suppressing-turnout#stream/0, accessed May 21,
2017.

p. 118: "7 percent of Americans" and "it is unclear that proof of citizenship": Chelsie Bright, "Kris Kobach and Kansas' SAFE Act," *The Conversation*, July 26, 2017, theconversation.com/kris-kobach-and -kansas-safe-act-81314, accessed December 8, 2017.

p. 118: "pure speculation": Amrit Cheng, "If You Care About the Right to Vote, Here Are Six Things You Need to Know About Kris Kobach," ACLU, May 17, 2017, /if-you-care-about-right-vote-here-are -six-things-you, accessed May 19, 2017.

p. 118: "Brown was truly" and "scant evidence": Cheng, "If You Care About the Right to Vote."

p. 118: "block[ed] 18,000": Stern, "The Presidential Advisory Commission on Election Mendacity."

p. 119: "a national move . . . weed out duplicates": Pennsylvania Department of State, "The Interstate Crosscheck Program: Things You Should Know."

p. 119: Lincoln L. Wilson's ordeal: Strauss, "Kris Kobach Came After Me for an Honest Mistake."

p. 120: "meaning . . . before Election Day": Palast, "The GOP's Stealth War Against Voters."

p. 120: Texas's attempt to purge about 80,000 voters and "weak": Corrie MacLaggan, "Texas Voter Purge Lawsuit Ends with Clarification Memo on Process for Clearing Rolls," *Huffington Post*, October 3, 2012, www.huffingtonpost.com/2012/10/03/texas-voter-purge -lawsuit_n_1937564.html, accessed May 17, 2017.

p. 120: "flagged close to half a million voters": Palast, "The GOP's Stealth War Against Voters."

pp. 120–21: 2016 purges in Arizona, Michigan, and North Carolina: "Voting Is for White People: The Origins of Crosscheck," Medium.com, April 29, 2017, https://medium.com/@SIIPCampaigns /voting-is-for-white-people-the-origins-of-crosscheck-c91d5d4532cc, accessed July 19, 2017.

pp. 121–22: "exactly zero" and "shocked . . . 27 states": Palast, "The GOP's Stealth War Against Voters."

p. 122: "infected with racial and ethnic bias": Sue Sturgis, "How Trump's New 'Election Integrity' Appointee Has Unleashed Chaos on Elections in the South," *Facing South*, May 17, 2017, https://www.facingsouth.org/2017/05/how-trumps-new-election-integrity-appointee-has-unleashed-chaos-elections-south, accessed May 19, 2017.

p. 122: on last names and percentages: Palast, "The GOP's Stealth War Against Voters."

p. 122: "Roughly 14 percent": Charles D. Ellison, "The GOP Keeps Quietly Purging Black Voters—and Democrats Aren't Doing Anything About It," *The Root*, May 24, 2017, www.theroot.com/the-gop-keeps-quietly-purging-black-voters-and-democrat-1795474628, accessed April 13, 2018.

p. 122: "Kobach is Jim Crow walking": Charles P. Pierce, "Kris Kobach's Voter Fraud Commission Is Definitely a Fraud," *Esquire*, October 10, 2017, www.esquire.com/news-politics/politics/a12819768/trump-kobach-voter-fraud-commission/, accessed October 10, 2017.

13. A SHAM AND A SCAM

p. 126: *New York Times* editorial: "The Bogus Voter-Fraud Commission," editorial, *New York Times*, July 22, 2017, www.nytimes.com/2017/07/22/opinion/sunday/the-bogus-voter-fraud-commission.html, accessed July 23, 2017.

p. 126: "voter registration takes forethought": Ben Jacobs, "Controversial Rightwing Activist to Join Trump's Election Integrity Commission: J. Christian Adams Has Led Lawsuits Against Jurisdictions with Large Minority Populations in Effort to Purge Voter Rolls," *Guardian*, July 11, 2017, www.theguardian.com/us-news/2017/jul/11/trump-election-integrity-commission-j-christian-adams?CMP=twt_gu, accessed July 11, 2017.

p. 126: "Obama Administration was attempting": Ifill, "President Trump's Election Integrity Commission Is Illegal and Unconstitutional—That's Why We Filed a Lawsuit"; Pema Levy, "Trump Election Commissioner Used Dubious Data to Allege an 'Alien Invasion,'" *Mother Jones*, July 18, 2017, www.motherjones.com/politics/2017/07/trump-election-commissioner-used-dubious-data-to-allege-an-alien-invasion/, accessed July 18, 2017.

p. 127: "window dressing": John Wagner, "Trump's Voter Fraud Commission Proves a Magnet for Controversy," *Washington Post*, September 16, 2017, www.washingtonpost.com/politics/trumps-voter -fraud-commission-proves-a-magnet-for-controversy/2017/09/15 /1e013fa2-9a30-11e7-82e4-f1076f6d6152_story.html, accessed September 17, 2017.

p. 128: "you are all about": Soibangla to FN-OVP-Election Integrity Staff, email, June 29, 2017, www.whitehouse.gov/sites/whitehouse.gov /files/docs/comments-received-june-29-through-july-11-2017.pdf, accessed July 14, 2017.

p. 128: "This commission is": Charlie Ticotsky to FN-OVP- Election Integrity Staff, email, June 29, 2017, www.whitehouse.gov/sites /whitehouse.gov/files/docs/comments-received-june-29-through-july-11 -2017.pdf, accessed July 14, 2017.

p. 128: "You have no right": Stephen Lehew to FN-OVP-Election Integrity Staff, email, June 29, 2017, www.whitehouse.gov/sites /whitehouse.gov/files/docs/comments-received-june-29-through-july-11 -2017.pdf, accessed July 14, 2017.

p. 128: "choice of this location": Jeffrey Toobin, "Trump's Voter- Fraud Commission Heads to New Hampshire," *New Yorker*, September 12, 2017, www.newyorker.com/news/daily-comment/trumps-voter-fraud -commission-heads-to-new-hampshire, accessed September 12, 2017.

p. 129: "a pivotal, close . . . in the state": Kris W. Kobach, "Exclusive—Kobach: It Appears That Out-of-State Voters Changed the Outcome of the New Hampshire U.S. Senate Race," *Breitbart*, September 7, 2017, /big-government/2017/09/07/exclusive-kobach-out-of- state-voters-changed-outcome-new-hampshire-senate-race/, accessed December 10, 2017.

p. 129: "baseless allegations": "Kris Kobach and His 5,313 Fraudulent Voters," editorial, *New York Times*, September 11, 2017, /2017/09/11/opinion/kris-kobach-fraudulent-voters.html, accessed September 11, 2017.

p. 129: "That kind of recklessness": Mark Joseph Stern, "Trump Voter Fraud Commission Halts Data Collection amid Torrent of Lawsuits and Complaints," *Slate*, July 10, 2017, www.slate.com/news-and-politics /2017/07/trump-voter-fraud-commission-halts-data-collection-amid -lawsuits.html, accessed July 10, 2017.

p. 129: "no preconceived notions" and "prominent . . . voter fraud": Lauren Rosenblatt, "Trump and Pence Defend Voter Fraud Panel at First Meeting," *Los Angeles Times*, July 19, 2017, www.latimes.com /politics/la-na-pol-trump-voting-commission-20170719-story.html, accessed December 11, 2017.

p. 130: "deter people": Pema Levy and Ari Berman, "Background Checks for Voting Get Floated at Trump Election Commission Meeting," September 12, 2017, www.motherjones.com/politics/2017/09/background -checks-for-voting-get-floated-at-trump-election-commission-meeting/, accessed September 12, 2017.

p. 130: "are playing a very serious": Steven Rosenfeld, "The Republican Effort to Rig Elections," Portside, September 16, 2017, www .portside.org/print/2017-09-16/republican-effort-rig-elections, accessed September 16, 2017.

p. 130: "there's a more-than-20-point": Noah Gordon, "Americans' Deep Racial Divide on Trusting the Police: It Isn't Just Ferguson—Polling Shows That Black Americans Are Wary of Law Enforcement Across the Nation, While Whites Are More Likely to Trust Officers," *Atlantic*, August 20, 2014, www.theatlantic.com/politics/archive /2014/08/americans-deep-racial-divide-on-trusting-the-police/378848/, accessed December 11, 2017.

14. "A NATIONAL CHAMPION"

p. 133: "African Americans represent": NAACP, "Criminal Justice Fact Sheet," www.naacp.org/criminal-justice-fact-sheet/, accessed December 11, 2017.

p 134: On 3.1 million disenfranchised: Jean Chung, "Felony Disenfranchisement: A Primer," The Sentencing Project, https://www .sentencingproject.org/publications/felony-disenfranchisement-a-primer/, accessed July 11, 2019.

p. 134: "the national champion": Alexander Clinton, "How one Floridian—and 1.7 million others—lost the right to vote," November 1,

2016, https://www.miamiherald.com/news/local/community/broward
/article111783547.html, accessed April 1, 2019.

p. 134: "Nearly one-third of those": Conor Friedersdorf, "Will
Florida Banish the Ghost of Jim Crow? The State Still Disenfranchises
More of Its Eligible Voters Than Any Other—But This Year, It Has the
Chance to Change That," Atlantic, October 3, 2017, www.theatlantic
.com/politics/archive/2017/10/florida-felon-disenfranchisement/541680/,
accessed December 11, 2017.

p. 135: "restored rights to": Florida Center for Investigative
Reporting, "How This Floridian Lost His Voting Rights."

**p. 136: "how they keep their voter rolls" and "voter roll
maintenance":** Vanita Gupta, "The Voter Purges Are Coming," *New
York Times*, July 19, 2017, www.nytimes.com/2017/07/19/opinion/donald
-trump-voting-rights-purge.html, accessed July 19, 2017.

PART FOUR: RIGGING THE RULES

15. ELBRIDGE GERRY'S SALAMANDER

p. 141: "flawed democracy": "Declining Trust in Government Is
Denting Democracy: According to a New Index, America's Democracy
Score Deteriorated in 2016," *Economist*, January 25, 2017, www.economist
.com/graphic-detail/2017/01/25/declining-trust-in-government-is-denting
-democracy, accessed January 4, 2018.

**p. 141: "no longer considered to be a fully functioning
democracy":** Andrew Reynolds, "North Carolina Is No Longer
Classified as a Democracy," *News and Observer*, December 22, 2016, www
.newsobserver.com/opinion/op-ed/article122593759.html, accessed
December 31, 2017.

p. 142: "political robbery": Cliff Sloan and Michael
Waldman,"History Frowns on Partisan Gerrymandering," *Washington
Post*, October 1, 2017, www.washingtonpost.com/opinions/history
-frownson-partisan-gerrymandering/2017/10/01/a6795fca-a491-11e?-ade1
-76d061d56efa_story.html, accessed October 6, 2017.

p. 143: "packing": *Shaw v. Reno*, 509 US 630 (1993).

p. 144: "white supremacy": "Ross Barnett, Segregationist, Dies;
Governor of Mississippi in 1960's," *New York Times*, November 7, 1987,

www.nytimes.com/1987/11/07/obituaries/ross-barnett-segregationist-dies
-governor-of-mississippi-in-1960-s.html, accessed January 4, 2018.

**p. 145: "The legislators devised a reapportionment plan . . .
guaranteed a victory":** Minion K. C. Morrison, *Aaron Henry of
Mississippi: Inside Agitator* (Fayetteville: University of Arkansas, 2015), 65.

p. 145: "roughly two-thirds": C-Span, "Landmark Cases: *Baker v.
Carr*," landmarkcases.c-span.org/Case/10/Baker-V-Carr, accessed
January 1, 2018.

pp. 145–46: "made no apportionment . . . of their votes": *Baker
v. Carr*, supreme.justia.com/cases/federal/us/369/186/case.html, accessed
January 1, 2018.

p. 146: "political . . . further delay": *Baker v. Carr.*

p. 146: "one person, one vote": *Reynolds v. Sims*, 377 US 533 (1964).

p. 147: "as if they were drawn": Sarah Koenig, "Congressional
Districts Fought in Federal Suit," *Baltimore Sun*, June 19, 2002.

p. 147: "look like a picnic": Charles S. Bullock III, *Redistricting: The
Most Political Activity in America* (Lanham, MD: Rowman Littlefield, 2010),
1–2.

**p. 147: "For the next decade" and on the thirteen of thirty
seats:** Charles S. Bullock III, *Redistricting: The Most Political Activity in
America* (Lanham, MD: Rowman Littlefield, 2010), 1–2.

p. 147: "knee-capping": Robert Draper, "The League of Dangerous
Mapmakers," *Atlantic*, October 2012, www.theatlantic.com/magazine
/archive/2012/10/the-league-of/309084/, accessed July 26, 2017.

p. 148: "prominent national figures . . . plans elsewhere":
Vieth v. Jubelirer, 541 US 267 (2004).

p. 149: "elections do not matter": Brief of Amici Curiae, the
American Civil Liberties Union, and the Brennan Center for Justice at
NYU School of Law in Support of Appellants, *Vieth v. Jubelirer*, 541 US
267 (2004).

p. 150: "is not simply": Anthony J. McGann, Charles Anthony
Smith, Michael Latner, and Alex Keena, *Gerrymandering in America: The
House of Representatives, the Supreme Court, and the Future of Popular Sovereignty*
(New York: Cambridge University Press, 2016), 7.

16. OF THE TEXAS GLOCK, THE GEORGIA FLAT-CAT ROAD KILL, AND OTHER ABERRATIONS

p. 153: "brute-force, computer-driven gerrymandering":
Kevin Drum, "Computers Have Revolutionized Gerrymandering. The Supreme Court Should Take Notice," *Mother Jones*, February 26, 2017, motherjones.com/kevin-drum/2017/02/computers-have-revolutionized
-gerrymandering-supreme-court-should-take-notice, accessed February 26, 2017.

pp. 153–54: "Exceptionally smart . . . stronghold" and "more Americans lived in": "Electoral Competitiveness in Michigan," Ballotpedia, April 2015, ballotpedia.org/Electoral_competitiveness_in
_Michigan, accessed December 29, 2017.

p. 154: "pack[ed] . . . asymmetry": Sam Wang and Brian Remlinger, "Can Math Stop Partisan Gerrymandering," *Los Angeles Times*, May 5, 2017, www.latimes.com/opinion/op-ed/la-oe-wang
-remlinger-gerrymandering-20170505-story.html, accessed May 21, 2017.

p. 154: "there is a 20%": McGann et al., *Gerrymandering in America*, 4.

p. 155: "wasted votes and silenced voices": Amicus Curiae Brief of Senators John McCain and Sheldon Whitehouse in Support of Appellees, *Gill v. Whitford*, US Supreme Court, No. 16-1161 (2017).

p. 155: "Citizens can't just vote": Michael Li and Thomas Wolf, "5 Things to Know About the Wisconsin Partisan Gerrymandering Case," Brennan Center for Justice, June 9, 2017, www.brennancenter.org/blog/5
-things-know-about-wisconsin-partisan-gerrymandering-case, accessed June 17, 2017.

p. 156: "party's willingness to use race": Olga Pierce and Kate Rabinowitz, " 'Partisan' Gerrymandering Is Still About Race," ProPublica, October 9, 2017, www.propublica.org/article/partisan
-gerrymandering-is-still-about-race, accessed October 9, 2017.

p. 157: "In other words . . . lavishly brazen maps": Draper, "The League of Dangerous Mapmakers."

p. 157: "white Republicans were awarded": Ari Berman, "Texas's Redistricting Maps and Voter-ID Law Intentionally Discriminated Against Minority Voters," *The Nation*, March 13, 2017, www.thenation.com/article

/texass-redistricting-maps-and-voter-id-law-intentionally-discriminated
-against-minority-voters/, accessed May 21, 2017.

p. 157: "Current voting maps erode": Colin Allred, "Voter
Suppression: How the Texas GOP 'Packed and Cracked' Districts to
Dilute Minorities' Voting Rights," *Dallas Morning News,* July 21, 2017,
https://www.dallasnews.com/opinion/commentary/2017/07/21/texas
-gop-packed-cracked-districts-dilute-minorities-voting-rights, accessed
July 21, 2017.

17. GILL V. WHITFORD

p. 159: "create . . . nondisclosure agreements": Thomas Wolf,
"Bringing Whitford into Focus," Brennan Center for Justice, August 8,
2017, www.brennancenter.org/blog/bringing-whitford-focus, accessed
August 9, 2017.

p. 161: "gerrymander is simply": Ian Milhiser, "The Most Exciting
Attack on Partisan Gerrymandering in Over a Decade," ThinkProgress,
April 18, 2016, think-progress.org/the-most-exciting-attack-on-partisan
-gerrymandering-in-over-a-decade-68ae8b6b2e5e/, accessed June 19,
2017.

p. 162: "an efficiency gap . . . rose to 12.3%": "Politicians
Choosing Voters: The Supreme Court Ponders Whether Gerrymandering
Has Gone Too Far," *Economist,* https://www.economist.com/united-states
/2017/10/07/the-supreme-court-ponders-whether-gerrymandering-has
-gone-too-far, accessed March 28, 2019.

p. 163: on *Gill v. Whitford*: Oral Arguments, *Gill v. Whitford,*
No. 16-1161, October 3, 2017, www.supremecourt.gov/oral_arguments
/argument_transcripts/2017/16-1611_bpm1.pdf, accessed October 7,
2017, pp. 22–23, 50.

p. 164: " 'incentive' to vote . . . electoral effects": M. V. Hood
and Seth C. McKee, "Trying to Thread the Needle: The Effects of a
Redistricting in a Georgia Congressional District," *PS: Political Science and
Politics* 42, no. 4 (October 2009): 683.

18. MORE DIRTY TRICKS

p. 169: "The last person to cast": A. J. Vicens, "The Election in
Arizona Was a Mess," *Mother Jones,* March 24, 2016, https://www

.motherjones.com/politics/2016/03/arizona-primary-long-lines-voting
-restrictions/, accessed June 4, 2017.

p. 169: "discourage voting": Charles Stewart III and Stephen
Anslabehere, "Waiting to Vote," *Election Law Journal* 14, no. 1 (2015):
47–53.

p. 170: "habit-forming": Alan S. Gerber, Donald P. Green, and Ron
Shachar, "Voting May Be Habit-Forming: Evidence from a Randomized
Field Experiment,"*American Journal of Political Science* 47, no. 3 (July 2003):
540–50.

p. 170: "10 Florida precincts": Jaeah Lee, "Charts: How Minority
Voters Get Blocked at the Ballot Box. It's Not Just Voter ID Laws and
Other Restrictions That Stymie Black and Latino Voters," *Mother Jones*,
November 3, 2014, www.motherjones.com/politics/2014/11/charts
-black-latino-voters-machines-poll-workers/#, accessed December 24,
2017.

p. 172: "I guess I really": Stephanie Mencimer, "Even Without
Voter ID Laws, Minority Voters Face More Hurdles to Casting
Ballots," *Mother Jones*, November 3, 2014, www.motherjones.com
/politics/2014/11/minority-voters-election-long-lines-id/, accessed
June 14, 2017.

p. 172: "moving a polling place can affect": Moshe Haspel and
H. Gibbs Knotts, "Location, Location, Location: Precinct Placement
and the Costs of Voting," *Journal of Politics* 67, no. 2 (May 2005), 560–61,
565.

**p. 172: "subtler maneuver . . . white voters largely
unaffected" and "North Carolina's changes":** Zachary Roth,
"Study: North Carolina Polling Site Changes Hurt Blacks," MSNBC,
November 23, 2015, www.msnbc.com/msnbc/study-north-carolina
-polling-site-changes-hurt-blacks, accessed June 2, 2017.

p. 174: "When voter suppression": Kristina Torres, "Cost-
Cutting Moves Spur Fears About Reducing Access to Georgia Voters,"
Atlanta Journal-Constitution, October 11, 2016, www.politics.myajc.com
/news/state—regional-govt—politics/cost-cutting-moves-spur-fears
-about-reducing-access-georgia-voters/qu9llnbKd6dSl6yblbB68M/,
accessed December 16, 2017.

NOTES

PART FIVE: THE RESISTANCE

19. SWEET HOME ALABAMA?

p. 180: on sewage systems and 2011 UN report: Connor Sheets, "UN Poverty Official Touring Alabama's Black Belt: 'I Haven't Seen This' in the First World," December 8, 2017, www.al.com/news/2017/12 /un_poverty_official_touring_al.html, accessed January 23, 2018.

p. 180: Alabama's ranking in public health: "Best States: About Alabama," *U.S. News and World Report*, www.usnews.com/news/best-states /alabama, accessed January 24, 2018.

p. 180: on infant mortality: Amy Yurkanin, "Rate of Infant Death in Alabama Increased in 2016," AL.com, November 16, 2017, https://www .al.com/news/2017/11/rate_of_infant_death_in_alabam.html, accessed January 23, 2018.

p. 180: stats on education, poverty, unemployment, and quality of government: "Best States: About Alabama," *U.S. News and World Report*, www.usnews.com/news/best-states/alabama, accessed April 1, 2019.

p. 181: "conservative extremist": David Corn, "Watch Roy Moore, the Latest GOP Star, Argue for Criminalizing Homosexuality," *Mother Jones*, September 27, 2017, www.motherjones.com/politics/2017/09/watch -roy-moore-the-latest-gop-star-argue-for-criminalizing-homosexuality/, accessed December 29, 2017.

p. 181: "I think it was great at the time": Tim Murphy, "Roy Moore Is Strangely Nostalgic for Slavery Days," *Mother Jones*, December 7, 2017, www.motherjones.com/politics/2017/12/roy-moore-is-strangely -nostalgic-for-slavery-days/, accessed January 26, 2018.

p. 181: "sliver of hope": "After Moore's Alabama Win, Dems See Sliver of Hope in Jones," Access WDUN, September 27, 2017, accesswdun .com/article/2017/9/587437, accessed January 27, 2018.

20. OF ABORIGINES AND ILLITERATES

p. 183: "a poverty rate": Anna Claire Vollers, "Alabama Is 6th Poorest State in Nation; Poverty Rate at 40 Percent in Some Counties," July 3, 2017, www.al.com/news/2017/07/alabama_is_6th_poorest_state _i.html, accessed February 11, 2018.

p. 184: "Alabama voter turnout reached a shameful nadir":
Sherrilyn A. Ifill to Governor Robert Bentley et al., letter, October 2,
2015, www.naacpldf.org/press-release/one-day-a-month-is-not-enough
-says-ldf/, accessed January 11, 2018.

p. 184: "depress the turnout of black voters": Scott Douglas,
"The Alabama Senate Race May Have Already Been Decided," *New York
Times,* December 11, 2017, https://www.nytimes.com/2017/12/11/opinion
/roy-moore-alabama-senate-voter-suppression.html, accessed January 1,
2018.

p. 184: on blacks in public housing: NAACP LDF, "LDF Files
Lawsuit to Challenge Alabama's Racially Discriminatory Photo ID Law,"
press release, December 2, 2015, www.naacpldf.org/update/ldf-files
-lawsuit-challenge-alabama's-racially-discriminatory-photo-id-law,
accessed February 24, 2018.

p. 185: "The lack of clear": Sam Levine, "There Are Huge Obstacles
to Casting a Ballot in Alabama's Special Election," *Huffington Post,*
December 14, 2017, https://www.huffingtonpost.com/entry/alabama
-special-election-voter-id_us_5a2ee40ee4b04617543278f2, accessed
January 11, 2018.

p. 186: on Alabama's public transportation sytem: Ifill to
Bentley, letter, October 2, 2015.

**p. 186: "anybody can go any day of the week" and "Since
2013":** Tim Lockette, "Ala. Move to Close Drivers License Facilities
'Discriminatory': ACLU," *Chicago Tribune,* October 2, 2015, www
.chicagotribune.com/news/nationworld/ct-alabama-drivers-license
-facilities-20151002-story.html, accessed January 14, 2018.

**p. 186: "If you're too sorry or lazy . . . initiative to become a
registered voter in this state":** Nick Wing, "Alabama's Republican
Secretary of State Calls Voting a 'Privilege': Apparently Automatically
Giving People Their Constitutional Rights Would Also Be Offensive
to Civil Rights Leaders," *Huffington Post,* November 3, 2016, www
.huffingtonpost.com/entry/john-merrill-alabama_us
_581a4760e4b0c43e6c1dbadd, accessed February 10, 2018.

p. 187: "nearly 2 percent from 2010 to 2016": Sue Sturgis,
"Voting Restrictions Could Affect Alabama's Special U.S. Senate
Election," *Facing South,* October 5, 2017, www.facingsouth.org/2017/10

/voting-restrictions-could-affect-alabamas-special-us-senate-election, accessed January 1, 2018.

p. 187: "putting 340,162 people . . . federal and state law"; "never got [a postcard] . . . deeply flawed"; and "many voters": "Group Asks Alabama to Restore Voters to 'Active' Status: The Southern Poverty Law Center Is Asking Alabama's Secretary of State to Restore Thousands of People to Active Voter Status," *U.S. News and World Report*, August 18, 2017, www.usnews.com/news/best-states/alabama /articles/2017-08-18/groups-asks-alabama-to-restore-voters-to-active -status/, accessed February 11, 2018.

p. 188: "to establish white supremacy": Keyssar, *The Right to Vote*, 249.

p. 188: "250,000 otherwise qualified": Julie Ebenstein, "The Alabama Governor Just Signed a Bill That Will Restore Voting Rights to Thousands of Alabamians," ACLU, May 26, 2017, www.aclu.org/blog /voting-rights/criminal-re-enfranchisment/alabama-governor-just-signed- bill-will-restore-voting, accessed January 14, 2018.

p. 188: on gerrymandering: Mike Cason, "Federal Judges Rule Alabama Must Redraw Legislative Districts," January 20, 2017, https:// www.al.com/news/birmingham/2017/01/federal_judges_rule_alabama _mu.html, accessed January 28, 2018.

p. 189: "Voting has always been . . . anywhere else": David Leonhardt, "Voter Fraud in Alabama," *New York Times*, December 12, 2017, www.nytimes.com/2017/12/12/opinion/alabama-election-voter -fraud.html, accessed November 11, 2018.

p. 189: "getting rid of constitutional amendments": Andrew Kaczynski, "Roy Moore in 2011: Getting Rid of Amendments After 10th Would 'Eliminate Many Problems,'" CNN, December 11, 2017, https://edition.cnn.com/2017/12/10/politics/kfile-roy-moore-aroostook -watchmen/index.html, accessed January 11, 2018.

p. 190: "Southern Baptists control": Charles Bethea, "Why Roy Moore's Law-School Professor Nicknamed Him Fruit Salad," *New Yorker*, October 26, 2017, www.newyorker.com/news/news-desk/why-roy-moores -law-school-professor-nicknamed-him-fruit-salad, accessed December 29, 2017.

p. 190: "really just a masquerade for white supremacy":
Richard Fausset and Campbell Robertson, "Black Voters in Alabama
Pushed Back Against the Past," *New York Times*, December 13, 2017,
https://www.nytimes.com/2017/12/13/us/doug-jones-alabama-black
-voters.html, accessed January 11, 2018.

**p. 191: "one man, one vote" and "We knew enough about . . .
really responsible for the Selma movement":** Henry Hampton
and Steve Fayer, *Voices of Freedom: An Oral History of the Civil Rights Movement
from the 1950's Through the 1980's* (New York: Bantam Books, 1990), 213–14.

p. 191: "Unlike traditional get-out-the-vote campaigns": Vann R.
Newkirk II, "How Grassroots Organizers Got Black Voters to the Polls in
Alabama," *Atlantic*, December 19, 2017, www.theatlantic.com/politics
/archive/2017/12/sparking-an-electoral-revival-in-alabama/548504/,
accessed January 11, 2018.

**p. 192: "We're at a crossroad"; "healthcare, education"; and
"For us . . . what's on the ballot":** Debra Barfield Berry, "Rallies,
Leafleting and Door Knocking All Part of Effort to Urge Voters to Cast
Ballots in Alabama Senate Race," *USA Today*, December 10, 2017, www
.usatoday.com/story/news/politics/2017/12/10/rallies-leafleting-and
-knocking-doors-all-part-effortsto-urge-voters-cast-ballots-alabama-senate
-rac/938309001/, accessed January 11, 2018.

p. 192: "there's things": "President of Alabama NAACP
on Democrat Doug Jones' Win," *All Things Considered*, NPR,
December 13, 2017, www.npr.org/2017/12/13/570603424/president
-of-alabama-naacp-on-democrat-doug-jones-win, accessed January 11,
2018.

p. 193: "We have to do this": David Detmold, "African Americans
Hold the Key to Victory for Doug Jones in Alabama," *Free Press*,
December 11, 2017, freepress.org/article/african-americans-hold-key
-victory-doug-jones-alabama, accessed January 11, 2018.

**p. 193: on mailings telling people they couldn't vote because
of a past conviction; "Alabama voter registration form . . .
list of crimes that are disqualifying"; and "scared away from
filling out . . . excuse by liberal minions from around the
world":** Levine, "There Are Huge Obstacles to Casting a Ballot in
Alabama's Special Election."

p. 193: "674 Alabama citizens who voted": Kira Lerner, "Alabama Elections Chief Wants to Send Citizens to Prison for 5 Years for Voting: Up to 674 People Who Switched Parties Between the Primary and Runoff Could Be Charged with a Felony," ThinkProgress, October 25, 2017, www.thinkprogress.org/crossover-voting-alabama-9b0eda42de54/, accessed October 25, 2017.

p. 195: on *Breitbart*'s allegations: Aaron Klein, "Soros Army in Alabama to Register Convicted Felons to Vote Against Roy Moore," *Breitbart*, December 3, 2017, www.breitbart.com/big-government/2017/12 /03/soros-army-alabama-register-convicted-felons-vote-roy-moore/, accessed January 1, 2018.

p. 195: "spent three years . . . charge was not a 'moral turpitude' offense": Ebenstein, "The Alabama Governor Just Signed a Bill That Will Restore Voting Rights to Thousands of Alabamians."

p. 196: Spencer Trawick: Connor Sheets, "Thousands of Alabama Felons Register to Vote in Last-Minute Push," AL.com, November 27, 2017, www.al.com/news/2017/11/advocates_make_last-minute_pus.html, accessed January 1, 2018.

p. 196: "unstable, inept, inexperienced, and also unethical": John Bowden, "Ex-CIA Chief: Trump 'Unstable, Inept, Inexperienced, and Also Unethical,'" *The Hill*, March 3, 2018, thehill.com/homenews /administration/376547-ex-cia-chief-trump-unstable-inept-inexperienced -and-also-unethical, accessed March 3, 2018.

21. "SELMA, LORD, SELMA"

p. 199: "GOP dominance": Newkirk, "How Grassroots Organizers Got Black Voters to the Polls in Alabama."

p. 200: "defeat the Trump agenda": Indivisible, www.indivisible.org/, accessed February 24, 2018.

p. 200: " 'HIGH VOTER TURNOUT' LANGUAGE": "Alabama Update," Indivisible Ventura, accessed March 20, 2019. Emphasis in original.

p. 200: "We had a lot of": David Smith, " 'A Perfect Storm': How Liberal Millennials and African Americans Delivered a Stunning Alabama Result," *Guardian*, December 16, 2017, www.theguardian.com

/us-news /2017/dec/16/alabama-senate-election-doug-jones-roy-moore-donald-trump, accessed January 11, 2018.

p. 201: "Doors. Doors. Doors. Turn ya folk out": Will Drabold, "Black Women Fueled a Grassroots Movement in Alabama—and May Remake State Politics," *Mic*, December 14, 2017, mic.com/articles/186790 /black-women-fueled-a-grassroots-movement-in-alabama-and-may -remake-state-politics#.900c3k HfD, accessed January 11, 2018.

p. 201: "centered its efforts": Newkirk, "How Grassroots Organizers Got Black Voters to the Polls in Alabama."

p. 201: "dozens of students . . . cast a ballot": Drabold, "Black Women Fueled a Grassroots Movement in Alabama—and May Remake State Politics."

p. 201: "knocked on more than": "'A Perfect Storm': How Liberal Millennials and African Americans Delivered a Stunning Alabama Result."

p. 201: on the work of Righteous Vote: Drabold, "Black Women Fueled a Grassroots Movement in Alabama—and May Remake State Politics."

p. 202: "handed out several": Al Giordano (@AlGiordano), "1. Just spoke with a source in the Mobile (AL) County NAACP . . . ," Twitter, December 12, 2017, 10:58 a.m.

p. 202: "Transportation to the polls is a HUGE issue in Alabama": "Alabama Update," Indivisible Ventura. Emphasis in original.

p. 202: on Perman Hardy: Connor Sheets, "How a Former Sharecropper in an SUV Helped Drive Doug Jones to Victory in Alabama's Black Belt," AL.com, December 13, 2017, /how_a_former_ sharecropper_in_a.html, accessed March 3, 2018.

p. 203: on BlackPAC's door knocking and paying organizers: Newkirk, "How Grassroots Organizers Got Black Voters to the Polls in Alabama."

p. 203: on Black Voters Matter crowdfunding: Drabold, "Black Women Fueled a Grassroots Movement in Alabama—and May Remake State Politics."

p. 203: "dozens of grants to smaller: Newkirk, "How Grassroots Organizers Got Black Voters to the Polls in Alabama."

p. 204: "specifically spent on": Ryan C. Brooks, "In the Lead-Up to Doug Jones' Win, Groups Actually Spent Millions Trying to Mobilize Black Voters," *BuzzFeed*, December 18, 2017, /in-the -lead-up-to-doug-joness-win-groups-actually-spent, accessed January 11, 2018.

p. 204: *Washington Post* story on Roy Moore: Stephanie McCrummen, Beth Reinhard, and Alice Crites, "Woman Says Roy Moore Initiated Sexual Encounter When She Was 14, He Was 32," *Washington Post*, November 9, 2017, www.washingtonpost.com /investigations/woman-says-roy-moore-initiated-sexual-encounter-when -she-was-14-he-was-32/2017/11/09/1f495878-c293-11e7-afe9 -4f60b5a6c4a0_story.html, accessed January 1, 2018.

p. 204: "spoke or messaged with": Charles Bethea, "Locals Were Troubled by Roy Moore's Interactions with Teen Girls at the Gadsden Mall," *New Yorker*, November 13, 2017, www.newyorker.com/news/news -desk/locals-were-troubled-by-roy-moores-interactions-with-teen-girls-at -the-gadsden-mall, accessed January 26, 2018.

p. 204: "I think the Republican Party . . . deserves better": Rosalind S. Helderman and David Weigel, "As Alabama Prepares to Vote, Republican Sen. Richard Shelby Says State 'Deserves Better' Than Moore," *Washington Post*, December 10, 2017, /as-alabama-prepares-to -vote-republican-sen-richard-shelby-says-state-deserves-better-than -moore/, accessed February 27, 2018.

p. 205: "Democratic operation": Jess Bidgood, "In Race Against Roy Moore, Democratic Candidate Is Mostly on His Own," *New York Times*, November 19, 2017, www.nytimes.com/2017/11/19/us/jones -alabama-democrats.html, accessed April 17, 2018.

p. 205: "about health care and jobs and infrastructure": Kira Lerner, "Black Alabamians Discuss Their Decisive Role in Doug Jones' Victory: 'That's the Power of the Sister Vote,'" *ThinkProgress*, December 13, 2017, think-progress.org/black-voters-alabama-election -067d73324dcc/, accessed January 11, 2018.

p. 205: "we saw numerous examples": *Roland Martin News One Now*, transcript, December 21, 2017.

p. 206: "received about 300 calls": Brian Lawson, "Alabama NAACP President Says He Expects Voter Turnout to Be Higher Than

25 Percent," WHNT, December 12, 2017, whnt.com/2017/12/12/__
trashed-36/, accessed January 11, 2018.

p. 206: "shortage of ballots . . . or check-in tables": Sherrilyn
Ifill, "Black Voters in Alabama Mattered Way Before Doug Jones Beat
Roy Moore," *Time*, December 19, 2017, time.com/5071404/alabama
-black-voters-doug-jones-roy-moore/, accessed January 11, 2018.

p. 206: "went into Montgomery . . . photo ID": *Roland Martin
News One Now*, transcript.

p. 207: "Three of them": Charles Bethea, "How the Trump
Resistance Went Pro in Alabama," *New Yorker*, December 15, 2017, www
.newyorker.com/news/news-desk/how-the-trump-resistance-went-pro-in
-alabama, accessed January 11, 2018.

**p. 208: "black people in Alabama punched above their
weight":** Ryan Brooks, "In the Lead-Up to Doug Jones' Win, Groups
Actually Spent Millions Trying to Mobilize Black Voters."

p. 208: Bernice King's tweet: Errol Louis, "Of Course, Selma Made
the Difference for Doug Jones," CNN, December 13, 2017, /opinions/
of-course-selma-made-the-difference-for-doug-jones-louis/index.html,
accessed January 14, 2018.

p. 208: "more than 40% of voters . . . a *Mic* analyst found":
Drabold, "Black Women Fueled a Grassroots Movement in Alabama—
and May Remake State Politics."

p. 209: "They never could see black people": Newkirk, "How
Grassroots Organizers Got Black Voters to the Polls in Alabama."

CONCLUSION

22. AT THE CROSSROADS

**pp. 213–14: "forc[e] Blacks to vote Killary . . . we'd surely be
better off without voting AT ALL":** Charles Pierce, "Mueller Has the
Goods Now, and Trump Knows It," *Esquire*, February 16, 2018, www
.esquire.com/news-politics-politics/a18212230/what-mueller-indictments
-mean/, accessed February 16, 2018.

**p. 214: "They would say things like . . . 'not showing up to
vote' ":** Jerry Zremski, "Russian Trolls Pushed Rally in Buffalo—Then

Urged Blacks Not to Vote," *Buffalo News*, March 10, 2018, www
.buffalonews.com/2018/03/10/russian-trolls-pushed-rally-in-buffalo-and
-urged-blacks-not-to-vote/, accessed March 11, 2018.

**p. 214: "They used the 'voter fraud' fantasy as well" and
@TEN_GOP activity:** Pierce, "Mueller Has the Goods Now, and
Trump Knows It."

pp. 214–15: "Voter suppression hacked our democracy": Ari
Berman, "American Democracy Is Now Under Siege by Both Cyber-
Espionage and GOP Voter Suppression," *The Nation*, July 12, 2017, www
.thenation.com/article/american-democracy-is-now-under-siege-by-both
-cyber-espionage-and-gop-voter-suppression/, accessed March 11, 2018.

p. 215: on Oregon's 68,583 new voters: Hedrick Smith, "The
Oregon Idea—Make Voting Easy," *Bill Moyers*, October 19, 2016, www.bill
moyers.com/story/oregon-idea-make-voting-easy/, accessed March 6,
2018.

p. 215: on Oregon's new votes by the end of July 2016: Jonathan
Brater, "Update: Oregon Keeps Adding New Voters at Torrid Pace,"
Brennan Center for Justice, August 19, 2016, www.brennancenter.org
/analysis/update-oregon-keeps-adding-new-voters-torrid-pace, accessed
March 15, 2018.

p. 215: on Oregon's voter turnout in 2016: Sean McElwee, Brian
Schaffner, and Jesse Rhodes, "How Oregon Increased Voter Turnout
More Than Any Other State," *The Nation*, July 27, 2017, www.thenation
.com/article/how-oregon-increased-voter-turnout-more-than-any-other
-state/, accessed March 6, 2018.

p. 215: on California's 2014 voter turnout: Lonnie Wong,
"California Looks at Colorado Voter Reform Model," Fox 40, May 27,
2015, https://fox40.com/2015/05/27/california-looks-at-colorado-voter
-reform-model/, accessed March 4, 2018.

p. 215: "boost turnout 7 to 14 percentage points": Nicole Flatow,
"Colorado Legislature Passes Major Voting Rights Expansion Bill,"
ThinkProgress, May 2, 2013, https://thinkprogress.org/colorado-legislature
-passes-major-voting-rights-expansion-bill-9de254d63e15/, accessed
March 2, 2018.

p. 216: "There is no reason": Smith, "The Oregon Idea—Make
Voting Easy."

p. 217: "15 days before an election . . . turnout": Keith Brekhus, "Democratic Led Minnesota Senate Approves Expanding Early Voting and Voting Rights," *Politicus*, May 12, 2015, www.politicususa.com/2015 /05/12/democratic-led-minnesota-senate-approves-expanding-early -voting-voting-rights.html, accessed March 6, 2018.

p. 219: "Latinos make up": Will Drabold, "How Cities Are Bypassing States to Explore Registering Hundreds of Thousands to Vote," *Mic*, January 5, 2018, https://mic.com/articles/187178/how-cities-are -bypassing-states-to-explore-registering-hundreds-of-thousands-to-vote# .n3SpuKTkz, accessed March 2, 2018.

p. 220: "When more citizens participate": New Mexico Senate Democrats, "New Mexico Senate Passes Legislation to Greatly Expand Voter Registration Time Period," KRWG, March 1, 2017, www.krwg.org /post/new-mexico-senate-passes-legislation-greatly-expand-voter -registration-time-period, accessed March 9, 2018; New Mexico Legislature, "2018 Regular Session—SB224," www.nmlegis.gov /Legislation/Legislation?chamber=S&legtype=B&legno=224&year=18& AspxAutoDetectCookieSupport=1, accessed March 18, 2018.

p. 220: "We know that when voters": Mary Spicuzza, "Milwaukee to More Than Double Early Voting Sites for 2018 Elections," *Milwaukee Sentinel Journal*, November 15, 2017, www.jsonline.com/story/news/local /milwaukee/2017/11/15/milwaukee-more-than-double-early-voting-sites -2018-elections/867191001/, accessed March 4, 2018.

PHOTOGRAPH CREDITS

INDEX

District courts, 36
DMV. *See* Department of Motor
    Vehicles
Dobynes, O. C., 48
DOJ. *See* Justice, Department of
Double V Campaign, 23
Douglas, Scott, 184
Douglas, William O., 59
Drabold, Will, 201, 208–209
Draper, Robert, 157
Driver's licenses
    automatic voter registration
        with, 215
    birth certificates needed for, 81,
        83
    distribution of offices for getting,
        83, 94, 185–186
    number of Americans without,
        76
    in voter ID laws, 67, 75–76, 81,
        94, 185–186
"Driving While Brown" laws, 115
Drugs, War on, 133–134
Drum, Kevin, 153
Dukakis, Michael, 101
Durable partisan effect, 162
Durbin, Dick, 216

Early voting
    expansion of, 217
    limits on availability of, 108,
        170–172
    long voting lines and, 170
Ebenstein, Julie, 195
Economist Intelligence Unit, 141
Education, of black children
    desegregation of, 30–31, 40–41
    underfunding of, 6, 40
Efficiency gap, in redistricting,
    161–165
Eisenhower, Dwight, 31, 32, 33
Election Assistance Commission,
    75
Elections. *See* Midterm elections;
    Presidential election; Primary
    elections; Special election
Electoral Integrity Project, 141

Equal protection clause of Fourteenth
    Amendment, 18, 53, 146
Esquire (magazine), 214
Exact Match program, *112*, 113–114

Facebook, in presidential election of
    2016, 214
Facing South (magazine), 187
False equivalencies, 76
Faulk, Kent, 93
Federal Bureau of Investigation
    (FBI), 25
Federal court system, structure of, 36
Felony disenfranchisement, 133–136
    in Alabama, 188, 193–196
    racial discrimination in, 133–134
Fifteenth Amendment
    passage of, 3
    and primary elections, 17, 19–21
The Fight to Vote (Waldman), 35
Florida
    early voting in, 171
    felony disenfranchisement in,
        134–136
    long voting lines in, 170
    poll taxes in, 14
    presidential election of 2000 in,
        52–53, 69, 72–73
    racial violence in, 23
    voter registration drives in, 173
Folsom, Jim, 8
Ford, Gerald, 69
Fourteenth Amendment
    equal protection clause of, 18,
        53, 146
    and gerrymandering, 146, 163
    passage of, 3
    and primary elections, 18–21
    and recount in presidential
        election of 2000, 53
Fraud. *See* Voter fraud
Freedom riders, 179
Frohling, Richard G., 79
Frost, Martin, 147
Fulton County (Georgia), voter ID
    laws and, 84
Fund, John, *Stealing Elections*, 84

Racial gerrymandering
  in Alabama, 188–189
  goal of, 143
  vs. partisan gerrymandering,
    143, 156
Racial segregation in schools,
  30–31, 40–41
Racial violence, 23–26
  in Civil Rights Movement,
    33–34, 179–180
  in primary elections, 24–25
  in response to school
    desegregation, 30–31
  Soviet Union on, 30–31
  against veterans, 24–25
Reagan, Ronald, 56
Receipts, for poll taxes, 13
Recession of 2008, 87
Reconstruction, 3–4
Recounts, in presidential election of
  2000, 53–54, *68*, 72–73
Reeb, James, 34
Registration. *See* Voter registration
Rehnquist, William, 55–56
Representation, proportional, 161,
  164
Republican Party. *See also specific
  politicians and strategies*
  demographic composition of, xii,
    54, 156
  Latino supporters of, 54
  in midterm elections of 2010, 88,
    150
  in one-party system of South, 17
  as party of Lincoln, 17
  reaction to Obama's election,
    87–88
  state governments controlled by,
    153
Restoration clinics, 194–195
Reuters, 107
Reynolds, Sean, 67
Rhode Island, automatic voter
  registration in, 216
The Right to Vote (Keyssar), 43, 54,
  55
Righteous Vote, 201

Roberts, John
  on gerrymandering, 164
  Rehnquist's influence on, 55–56
  on Voting Rights Act, 42–43, 53,
    55–59
Robinson, Julie, 118
Rodriguez, Xavier, 156
Rokita, Todd, 79
Rolling Stone (magazine), 107
Rome (Georgia), annexation scheme
  in, 55–56
Romney, Mitt, 105
The Root (magazine), 122
Ross, Scot, 220
Roth, Zachary, 172
Russia, in presidential election of
  2016, *212*, 213–215, 219

SAFE. *See* Secure and Fair Elections
Same-day voter registration, 215,
  217
Sanders, Hank, 35, 43–44
SB. *See* Senate Bill
Scalia, Antonin, 149–150, 156, 166
School desegregation
  education of black children
    during, 40–41
  racial violence in response to,
    30–31
Scott, Rick, *132*, 135–136
SEA. *See* Senate Enrolled Act
Seattle (Washington), voter fraud in,
  77
Secure and Fair Elections (SAFE)
  Act of 2011 (Kansas), 116–117
Segregation. *See* Racial segregation
Selma (Alabama)
  Civil Rights Movement in,
    33–34, 179–180
  in Senate special election of
    2017, 208–209
Senate, US. *See* Congress, US
Senate Bill (SB) 14 (Texas), 94–95
Senate Enrolled Act (SEA) 483
  (Indiana), 79–82
Senate Majority PAC, 203
Sentencing Project, 134